AMERICAN TIGER 6

STUDENT'S BOOK

macmillan education

Carol Read • Mark Ormerod

Welcome back to the Tiger Tracks Social Learning Network

Lessons 1 & 2

1 01:02 **Listen and read.**

Welcome back to the Tiger Tracks Social Learning Network! This year, we:

- communicate with children from different English-speaking countries
- share ideas and opinions
- learn amazing facts about the world
- learn about different cultures
- do interesting and creative projects
- prepare for middle school

1

Hello. I'm Becky. I live in the United States. I'm 12 years old.

Character: scientific and techy
Interests: famous scientists and inventors
Ambitions: to be a doctor and work in a hospital

2

Hello. My name's Zoe. I come from Canada. I'm 11.

Character: sporty and artistic
Interests: the Olympic Games, track and field
Ambitions: to run in the Boston marathon

3

Hi there. My name's Florence. I'm from Jamaica. I'm 12 years old.

Character: scientific and creative
Interests: nutrition and cooking
Ambitions: to host a TV program about food from around the world

2 01:03 **Listen and repeat.** **Say and identify.**

A	B	C	D	E
100	104	365	825	999
1,000	1,005	1,440	2,500	5,555
10,000	12,700	22,880	99,005	100,000

3 01:04 **Listen and say which number.**

Why not play big numbers bingo?

4

Hi there. My name's Finn. I'm from Ireland. I'm 14 years old.

Character: artistic and imaginative
Interests: comic books, theater and movies
Ambitions: to write and direct a movie

5

Hello. I'm Kim. I live in England. I'm 12 years old.

Character: sporty and scientific
Interests: famous athletes and inventors
Ambitions: to be a firefighter and work at a fire station

6

Hello, everyone! My name's Ed. I'm from Wales. I'm 13 years old.

Character: musical and sporty
Interests: musical instruments and soccer
Ambitions: to play in a band and travel around the world

7

Hello there. I'm Scott. I live in New Zealand. I'm 12.

Character: sporty and adventurous
Interests: nature and geography
Ambitions: to learn to climb mountains

Can you find and name the countries the TTSLN visited in American Tiger 5?

4 Listen and say. Play *Who is it?*

01:05

She's creative. She's interested in cooking. She wants to host a TV program about good food.

5 Ask your friends. Tell the class.

What type of person are you?

What are you interested in?

What do you want to do in the future?

1 In your free time

AIMS

In this unit:

- I **name** and **talk about** free time activities.
- I **listen to** and **read** a success story *A talented boy*.
- I **talk about** what activities people like doing.
- I **find out about** Welsh and US culture.
- I **act out** inviting a friend to a concert in a role play.
- I **read about** different languages, and **write** and **present** a project.

Lesson 1

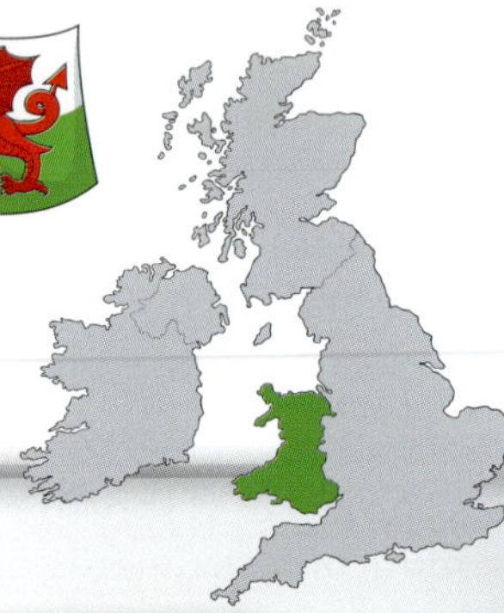

1 01:07 **Listen and say.**

Tiger Tracks SLN POST ✓

Hi. I'm Ed. I live in Cardiff, the capital of Wales. I go to a youth club. Guess which activities I do at the club. Which activities do you do?

1 
go to pop concerts

2 
do puzzles

3 
collect things

4 
play the drums

5 
juggle

6 
use the internet

7 
make things

8 
play chess

9 
go fishing

10 

practice a foreign language

2 01:08 **Listen and find out. Which activities does Ed do at the youth club? Now ask and talk about you.**

- Do you juggle in your free time?
- Yes, I very often do.
- Yes, I sometimes do.
- No, I never do.

3 01:09 **Listen and do the vocabulary quiz.**

To do this, you need a board but you don't need any dice. You need a king and a queen.

INTERNET TRACKS Look at a map of the UK. Find Cardiff. How far is it from Cardiff to London?

Lesson 2

4 Listen and read. 01:10

POST ✓

Here's some information about the youth club I go to. I think it's a great club. What do you think?

THE STREETWISE YOUTH CLUB

- Are you between 10 and 16 years old?
- Do you have a lot of free time?
- Do you like doing a lot of different activities?

If your answers are YES, YES, YES, then the Streetwise Youth Club is the place for you.

At the club, you can meet a lot of children. And you can choose from a variety of activities.

Playing sports and games

You can play chess, cards and many other games. You can play soccer, table tennis and many other sports. We organize competitions with other youth clubs in the area.

Collecting and making things

Many of our members are very creative. We collect old magazines, plastic bottles and old clothes, and we make things from these recycled objects.

Going on trips

On the weekend, we sometimes go on trips. We go to interesting museums and great pop concerts. We explore the wilderness around our town.

Learning new skills

At the Streetwise Youth Club you can learn new computer skills. You can also practice a foreign language or learn to play a musical instrument.

READING TIP Use the headings to help you find information quickly.

The Streetwise Youth Club is open every afternoon after school and all day on Saturday.
Membership: $10.00 a month. You can come once a week, twice a week, or every day of the week. You choose!

5 Answer the questions.

1 How old are members of the youth club?
2 How many sports are named in the text?
3 When is the youth club open?
4 Can you go to the youth club on Sunday?
5 How much does it cost to be a member of the youth club?

6 Work in groups. Remember and write.

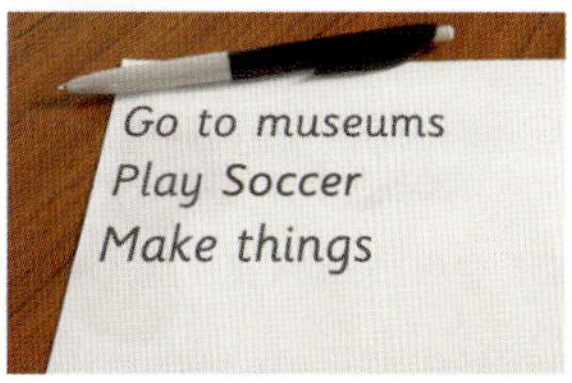

THINKING SKILLS
Remembering

TALK ABOUT IT!

7 Think and say.

I think going to a youth club is a good idea because you can meet other children.

INTERNET TRACKS Find out what you can see at the National Museum, Cardiff.

Lesson 3

8 01:12 **Listen to and read the story.**

This is a success story about some people I know at the Streetwise Youth Club. I hope you like it. POST ✓

A talented boy

- **What activity is David good at?**
- **What does David's brother do?**

9 **Read and say *True* or *False*. Correct the false sentences.**

1 David joins a chess club.
2 Liz and Benny like making things.
3 David doesn't like dancing.
4 David's brother is an art teacher.
5 The children decide to form a dance group.
6 One week later the children give a performance.

Tiger Values
Think about it!

Is it important to try new activities? Why?
Do you like trying new activities?

Do you know...?
There are many street dance groups in Wales. Some of the groups compete in the World Street Dancing Championship every year.

TALK ABOUT IT!

10 **Ask and say.**

1 Do you like the story? Why? / Why not?
2 What's your favorite part of the story?
3 Do you think it's easy to be a street-dance champion?
4 Do you like dancing?

Everyday phrases: learn and use!

Did you hear that?
That's amazing!
You're really good!
That's incredible!

Lesson 4

11 01:13 **Listen and read. Who does more sports?**

Julia

I **like going** to the youth club.

Julia is 15 years old and she's a member of the Streetwise Youth Club. She **likes going** to the club because she can see her friends. They **like using** the club computers to do their homework. Julia **doesn't like playing** table tennis, but she sometimes plays soccer. And she's learning to play the drums at the club. She **loves playing** the drums.

Anthony

I think the youth club is great.

Anthony is 12. He goes to the Streetwise Youth Club with his brother every Friday after school. They **like juggling**, and **playing** board games, soccer and table tennis at the club. Anthony **doesn't like playing** computer games, but he **likes using** the internet to find out about science. Anthony is also learning Chinese at the club with a boy from China. He **likes learning** foreign languages.

12 **Ask and answer.**

Does Julia like juggling?

No, she doesn't.

It doesn't say.

Yes, she does.

13 01:14 **Listen, repeat and learn.**

***like* + *...ing* (review and extension)**

I / You / We / They	like	swimming. juggling. playing chess.
He / She	likes	

I / You / We / They	don't like	swimming. juggling. playing chess.
He / She	doesn't like	

Do you	like	swimming? juggling? playing chess?	Yes,	I do.	No,	I don't.
Does he / she				he / she does.		he / she doesn't.

14 **Be a grammar detective! Look at page 7 in the AB.**

When there is a verb after *like*, what form of the verb do we use?

What are the short answers to questions beginning with *Do you like...?*

Can you find five examples of *like* + *...ing* in the story?

FAST TRACK GRAMMAR *Write five sentences about what you and your family like doing.*

Lesson 5

Sound track

15 01:16 **Listen and count the syllables. Identify the sentence stress.**

Do you like playing soccer?

No, I like playing basketball.

Do you like listening to pop music?

No, I like listening to classical music.

16 01:17 **Listen and say *True* or *False*. Correct the false sentences.**

17 **Play *Who am I thinking about?***

Is it a boy or a girl?

It's a boy.

Does he like doing puzzles?

No, he doesn't.

Does he like playing chess?

Yes, he does.

Are you thinking about Billy?

Yes, I am.

18 **Talk about you and your friends.**

TALK ABOUT IT!

I don't like playing computer games, but I love using the internet. My friend Paul likes taking photos.

FAST TRACK GRAMMAR *Write five sentences about what your friends like or don't like doing.*

Wales is a small country, but its culture is rich and varied. It has its own language, Welsh, and strong traditions in music and sports.

Lesson 6

19 01:19 **Listen and read.**

Welsh Culture

LANGUAGE

About 20% of Welsh people are bilingual. They speak English and Welsh. Welsh is a very old language, and people are making an effort to keep the language alive. At schools in Wales, all children have Welsh lessons. And most of the road signs in Wales are in both English and Welsh.

MUSIC

Wales is sometimes called 'the land of song'. Music is an important part of Welsh culture. Many pop stars and opera singers come from Wales, like Stereophonics, Tom Jones and Charlotte Church. But the country is especially famous for its male voice choirs. Many boys and men of all ages join choirs. They meet every week to practice. They sing songs in Welsh and in English.

SPORTS

People in Wales play many kinds of sports, but the national sport is rugby. Rugby is a very physical sport. In rugby, you can score goals and tries. You score a goal when you kick the ball between the other team's goal posts. You score a try when you put the ball on the ground behind the other team's goal line. There are men's rugby teams and women's rugby teams, too.

What is your country famous for?
Are people bilingual in your country?

20 **Read and guess.** 01:20 **Listen and say the answers.**

How much do you know about Wales? Do this culture quiz.

Culture quiz time: Wales

1. What's the capital of Wales? a) Cardiff b) Edinburgh c) Dublin
2. What's on the flag of Wales? a) a blue bird b) a yellow flower c) a red dragon
3. Which languages do many people speak? a) English and Welsh b) English and Spanish c) English and French
4. Which famous writer is from Wales? a) J.K. Rowling b) Enid Blyton c) Roald Dahl
5. Who is the patron saint of Wales? a) St George b) St David c) St Andrew
6. Which vegetable is the national symbol of Wales? a) the leek b) the carrot c) the potato

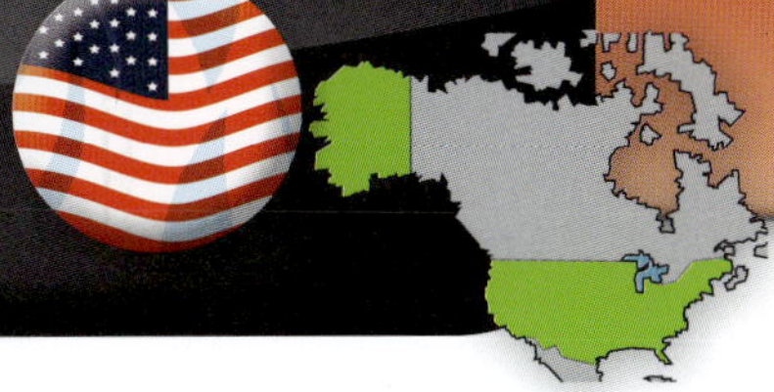

In the US there are many places to watch sports and pop concerts. AT&T Stadium is one of the most famous. POST ✓

Lesson 7

21 01:22 **Listen and read. Say *True* or *False*.**

1 AT&T Stadium is in Arlington, Texas.
2 It is the smallest American football stadium in the US and can seat 20,000 people.
3 It is the home field for the Dallas Cowboys.
4 In 2009, the stadium set a record for the most people to attend a concert.
5 The stadium hosts American football games for colleges and soccer games, too.
6 Famous singers such as Beyoncé, Taylor Swift, and the Jonas Brothers sometimes give concerts in the stadium.

Everyday chit-chat

! How to invite a friend to a concert

22 01:23 **Listen and repeat.**

1 
a stadium

2 
a pop concert

3 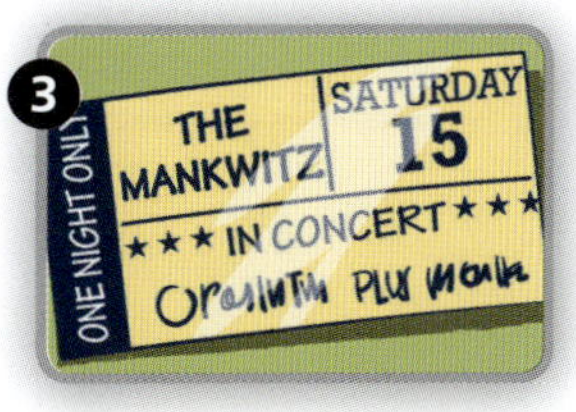

an extra ticket

4 
three fifteen

23 01:24 **Listen and read. Repeat.**

Carrie: Hello?
Becky: Hi, Carrie. It's Becky.
Carrie: Hi. How are you?
Becky: I'm fine, thanks. I'm calling to see if you're free on Saturday night.
Carrie: Yes, I am. Why?
Becky: Well, my family has tickets to see the Jonas Brothers, at AT&T Stadium.
Carrie: Wow! You're so lucky. The Jonas Brothers are my favorite pop group.
Becky: Well, would you like to see the concert with us? My brother has a bad cold, so we have an extra ticket.
Carrie: Oh yes. Wow! I'd love to! Just let me ask my dad.

Carrie: Hi, Becky. My dad says I can go. I'm so excited!
Becky: Good. We can pick you up from your house at three fifteen on Saturday afternoon.
Carrie: OK. That's great. Thank you, Becky.

24 **Do a role play.**

CLIL

Language

Lesson 8

Hi there! In Wales, a lot of people are bilingual. I speak English at home. At school, I speak Welsh, and I'm learning French, too. Here's an article from our school magazine. Two people talk about the languages they're learning.

POST

25 01:25 **Listen and read.**

Differences and similarities in languages

There are more than 6,000 different languages in the world. Some of these languages have similar vocabulary and grammar, but many are completely different.

For example:

- Some languages give nouns a gender. The nouns can be masculine, feminine or neutral. Other languages don't give nouns a gender.
- Some languages use letters of the Roman alphabet to write words. Other languages use symbols or characters instead of the Roman alphabet.
- Some languages don't conjugate verbs. Other languages have many different conjugations.

雨 the Chinese and Japanese character for 'rain'

How do you say 'Do you live in Wales?' in Welsh?

Ydych chi'n byw yng Nghymru?

People learning foreign languages

Harry. I'm learning Japanese because my brother lives in Japan. Some aspects of Japanese are easy. For example, there aren't any verb conjugations, and nouns don't have a gender. But reading and writing in Japanese is very difficult for me. There are thousands of different characters to learn. And when you read a sentence, you don't read it from left to right. You read it from top to bottom.

Vanessa. I'm English, but I live in Wales. I'm learning Welsh because I want to speak to my Welsh friends in Welsh. In English, nouns don't have a gender, so it's difficult for me to remember the gender of nouns in Welsh. And spelling Welsh words isn't easy. But I love speaking the Welsh language, and I'm very happy with my progress.

THINKING SKILLS
Comparing and contrasting

26 **Read and answer.**

1 Which language is written in characters?
2 Which language doesn't conjugate verbs?
3 Which language gives nouns a gender?
4 Which language do you read in a different direction?
5 What things do Harry and Vanessa think are difficult about learning a language?

27 **Play *Read and change.*** Bridge to ESO

There are more than 6,000 different languages in Europe.

Stop! It doesn't say Europe. It says the world.

28 **Think and say.** My world

What do you like about learning English?

What do you think is easy and difficult?

My words to remember

letters of the Roman alphabet   characters
gender   conjugate verbs   Japanese   Welsh

INTERNET TRACKS **Find out how to write the numbers 1 to 10 in Japanese characters.**

Project: Free-time survey

29 01:27 **Look at the graph. Listen and read.**

I asked 20 people at my school about the activities they like doing in their free time. Here are the results of my survey.

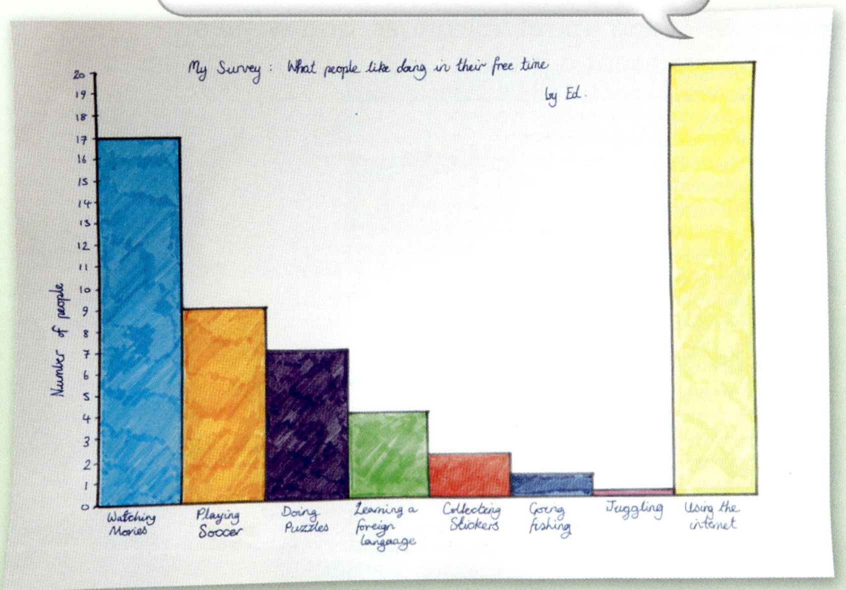

Yesterday, I presented this project in class. Which activities are very popular? Which activities are not popular? POST

I wasn't surprised to find out that our favorite activities are using the internet and watching movies. But I was very surprised to find out that nobody juggles in their free time. I love juggling. It's one of my favorite activities.

30 **Plan your project.**

THINKING SKILLS
Analyzing

1. **Write questions.**
2. **Interview people.**
3. **Draw your results.**
4. **Write and present your results.**

You can also present your results using a pie chart.

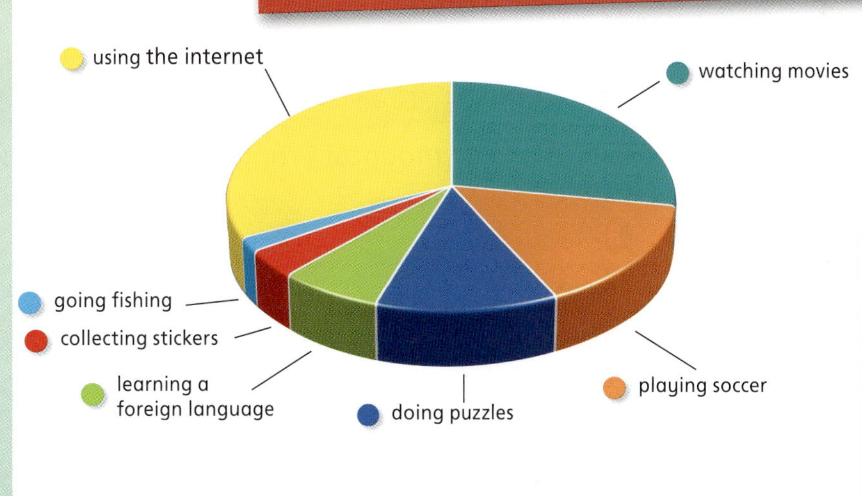

AB page 12

Do the Unit 1 Review and self-assessment (Activity Book page 12). Complete your *Progress Journal* for Unit 1.

2 Geographical wonders

AIMS

In this unit:

- I **name** and **describe** geographical features.
- I **listen to** and **read** a biography *Sir Edmund Hillary.*
- I **talk about** the highest and longest geographical features.
- I **find out about** New Zealand and US culture.
- I **act out** describing what I can see in a role play.
- I **read about** volcanoes, and **write** and **present** a project.

Lesson 1

1 01:29 **Listen and say.**

Tiger Tracks SLN POST ✓

Hi. My name's Scott. I'm from New Zealand. My country is famous for its beautiful landscapes. Which of these geographical features are there in New Zealand? Can you see them in your country?

1 
volcano

2 
glacier

3 
cliff

4 
waterfall

5 
mountain range

6 
cave

7 
rainforest

8 
desert

9 
island

10 
valley

2 01:30 **Listen and find out. Which geographical features are there in New Zealand?**

Now ask and talk about your country.

Are there any volcanoes in your country?

Yes, there are. | I'm not sure. | No, there aren't.

3 01:31 **Listen and do the vocabulary quiz.**

It's made of ice.
It moves very slowly.

INTERNET TRACKS Find out how far it is from New Zealand to Australia.

Lesson 2

4 Listen and read. 01:32

Here's a website about the POST incredible landscape of New Zealand! Which island do you think is more interesting to visit?

The natural beauty of New Zealand

READING TIP Don't worry about the pronunciation of place names.

New Zealand is a country in the Southern Hemisphere. It has two main islands. One is called North Island and the other is called South Island. There are many different areas of natural beauty to see on both islands.

North Island is 113,729 square kilometers. There are fantastic beaches on the west coast. There are rainforests where you can see rare plants and wildlife. There are mountains and there are a lot of volcanoes. The largest volcano is called Mount Ruapehu. It is 2,797 meters high and it is an active volcano. New Zealand's largest lake is on North Island. It is called Lake Taupo. And one of the most popular tourist attractions is the Waitomo Caves.

Waterfall in the Whirinaki Rainforest

Westland National Park

South Island is 151,215 square kilometers. It is more mountainous than North Island. The Southern Alps is a mountain range that starts in the north of South Island and finishes in the south. Mount Cook is in the Southern Alps. It is 3,754 meters high, and it is the highest mountain in New Zealand. Fiordland is the country's largest national park. You can see mountains, glaciers, valleys and lakes in the park. It is very popular with climbers and hikers.

THINKING SKILLS
Comparing

5 **Answer the questions.**

1 Which is bigger, North Island or South Island?
2 Which island has more mountains?
3 Where can you see New Zealand's largest lake?
4 What is the name of the largest national park?
5 What is the Southern Alps?

6 **Play a memory game.**

Where can you see caves?

On North Island!

7 **Choose and say.** TALK ABOUT IT!

I want to visit New Zealand because I want to see the volcanoes.

INTERNET TRACKS Find out what insect lives in the Waitomo Caves.

Lesson 3

8 Listen to and read the story.

01:34

POST ✓

This story is the biography of Sir Edmund Hillary, a famous climber from New Zealand. He lived from 1919 to 2008. His image is on the New Zealand $5 bill. He is one of my favorite people from history. Enjoy! ☺

Sir Edmund Hillary

- Why is Sir Edmund Hillary famous?
- Who saves his life in the story?

1 It is 1931. Edmund is eleven. On the train to school, he often reads adventure stories and books about explorers.

2 As a young man, Edmund climbs cliffs, mountains and volcanoes in New Zealand. He sometimes climbs with friends, but he often climbs alone.

3 It is 1953. Edmund is 33. He goes to Nepal to climb Mount Everest, the highest mountain in the world.

4 In the expedition to climb Mount Everest, there are 11 climbers, a journalist, a photographer, a doctor, and 350 porters to carry all the food and equipment. Edmund talks to Tenzing Norgay, a climber from Nepal.

9 **Read and answer the questions.**

1. What types of books does Edmund read as a boy?
2. When does Edmund go to Nepal?
3. How many porters are on the expedition to climb Everest?
4. Edmund nearly dies during the expedition. How?
5. How high is Mount Everest?
6. How long do Edmund and Tenzing stand on top of Everest?

Tiger Values
Think about it!

Is it sometimes important to work as a team? Why?

When do you work in a team?

5 The climbers begin their ascent. Edmund climbs with Tenzing. A rope connects them. It's extremely cold. And very windy.

6 During the expedition, Edmund falls through a crack in the ice. Tenzing reacts quickly and saves Edmund's life.

7 The climbers climb for six long weeks. At 7,900 meters the temperature is extremely cold. The oxygen is thin. Some of the climbers can't feel their feet. Some of them feel sick.

8 At 8,800 meters, Edmund and Tenzing are alone. They don't have much oxygen. And the last 50 meters are the most dangerous.

9 On May 29th at 11:30 a.m., Edmund and Tenzing are the first climbers in history to reach the top of Mount Everest. They are at 8,850 meters. They stand there for 15 minutes and look at the view. Edmund takes photos.

It is one of the most important moments in the history of climbing.

Do you know...?

After Tenzing Norgay and Edmund Hillary climbed Everest, journalists asked 'Who reached the top first?' They answered, 'We reached the top together, as a team.'

10 Ask and say.

TALK ABOUT IT!

1. Do you like the story? Why? / Why not?
2. What's your favorite part of the story?
3. Does anything in the story surprise you?
4. Do you want to climb Mount Everest?

Everyday phrases: learn and use!

It's good to see you.
It's extremely cold.
It's very windy.
We did it!

GRAMMAR TRACKS

Lesson 4

11 01:35 **Listen and read. Answer the questions in the first paragraph.**

Guinness World Records – a reference website

Which is **the highest** mountain in the world? Which is **the widest** river in the world? Which is **the smelliest** frog in the world? Which is **the most dangerous** shark in the world? When you ask questions like these, where do you find the answers? Do you look for the answers on the internet, or in an encyclopedia? Or do you look in a book called *Guinness World Records*?

Guinness World Records is a reference website. It contains information about **the highest**, **the smelliest**, **the hottest**, **the longest** and **the most exceptional** things in the world. For example, Mount Everest is **the highest** mountain in the world, the Sahara is **the hottest** desert, the Amazon is **the widest** river, and the Pacific is **the deepest** ocean.

The smelliest frog is the Venezuelan skunk frog. And **the most dangerous** shark in the world is the great white shark.

There are also *Guinness World Records* museums and a *Guinness World Records* book.

12 **Work in groups. Play *Team Reading Race*.**

Which | is | the | highest | mountain | in | the | world?

13 01:36 **Listen, repeat and learn.**

Superlative adjectives

I'm	tall.
You're	young.
He's	noisy.
She's	big.
It's	strange.
We're	intelligent.
They're	interesting.

I'm	the tallest			
You're	the youngest	person		
He's	the noisiest	place		the world.
She's	the biggest	animal	in	our class.
It's	the strangest			my family.
We're	the most intelligent	people		
They're	the most interesting	animals		

14 **Be a grammar detective! Look at page 17 in the AB.**

When do we use superlative adjectives?

How do we make superlative adjectives?

How many superlative adjectives can you find in the story?

FAST TRACK GRAMMAR *Write five sentences about your family using superlative adjectives.*

Lesson 5

15 01:38 **Listen and read. Identify two ways to pronounce *-est*.**

Sound track /est/ /ɪst/

This bird's n**est** isn't the cheap**est**, but it's the b**est**. It's the bigg**est** and the strong**est** and it's a nice place to r**est**.

16 01:39 **Look. Listen and answer the questions.**

Lia

Age: 13
Height: 1.47 meters
Character:

creative	✓✓✓
sporty	✓
musical	✓✓
scientific	✓

Stanley

Age: 11
Height: 1.45 meters
Character:

creative	✗
sporty	✓✓
musical	✗
scientific	✓✓✓

Tom

Age: 12
Height: 1.42 meters
Character:

creative	✓
sporty	✓
musical	✓✓✓
scientific	✗

Jane

Age: 14
Height: 1.43 meters
Character:

creative	✗
sporty	✓✓✓
musical	✗
scientific	✓✓

17 **Play *Who am I?***

Are you the youngest?
No, I'm not.
Are you the most musical?
No, I'm not.
Are you the sportiest?
Yes, I am.
You're Jane!
Yes, that's right.

18 **Talk about you and your friends.**

John is the youngest. Lisa is the most scientific.
Laura doesn't have the longest hair.

TALK ABOUT IT!

FAST TRACK GRAMMAR *Write five superlative sentences about the people in your class.*

The kiwi is a bird that lives in New Zealand. It is a symbol of my country. Many other birds also live in New Zealand. In fact, the country is sometimes called 'the land of birds'.

POST ✓

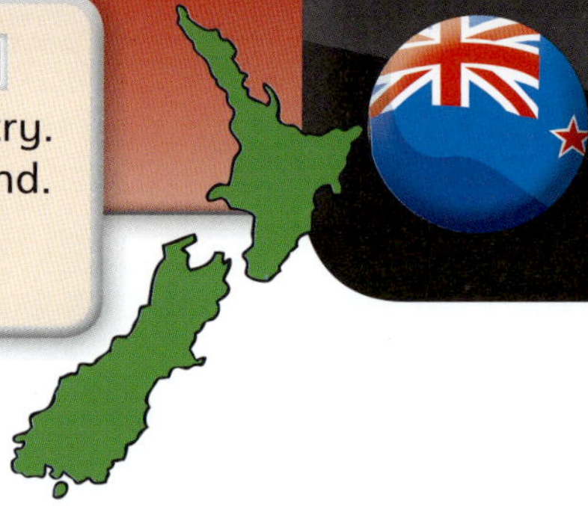

Lesson 6

19 01:40 **Listen and read.**

New Zealand, the Land of Birds

There are many animals in New Zealand that you cannot see anywhere else in the world. There are very rare types of spiders, dolphins, lizards and sea lions. But New Zealand is most famous for its birds. Many of these birds are unique to New Zealand because they are flightless birds. They cannot fly, so they cannot travel to other countries.

1 **The kakapo** is a type of parrot. It is the only flightless parrot in the world. The adults can weigh over three kilograms, so the kakapo is also the heaviest species of parrot in the world.

The blue penguin lives in many parts of New Zealand. There are 17 species of penguins in the world, and many of them live in New Zealand. The blue penguin has blue-gray feathers and it is the smallest species of penguin. It is about 30 cm long and it weighs about one kilogram.

2

The kiwi is a flightless bird with a very long beak. A kiwi is about the same size as a chicken. But a kiwi's egg is six times larger than a chicken's egg! The male kiwi incubates the egg and looks after it for about 80 days. 80 days! That's the longest incubation period of any bird in the world.

3

What species of birds live in your country? Are any of them flightless birds?

20 **Read and guess.** 01:41 **Listen and say the answers.**

POST ✓

Now it's my turn to give you a culture quiz on New Zealand. Are you ready?

Culture quiz time: New Zealand

1. What's the capital of New Zealand? **a)** Queensland **b)** Wellington **c)** Auckland
2. Who are the indigenous people of New Zealand? **a)** the Maoris **b)** the Aborigines **c)** the Inuits
3. What are the official languages of New Zealand? **a)** Maori and English **b)** English and French **c)** Maori and Spanish
4. What's the population of New Zealand? **a)** 4 million **b)** 14 million **c)** 24 million
5. What is New Zealand money called? **a)** euros **b)** dollars **c)** pounds
6. What are people from New Zealand sometimes called? **a)** penguins **b)** parrots **c)** kiwis

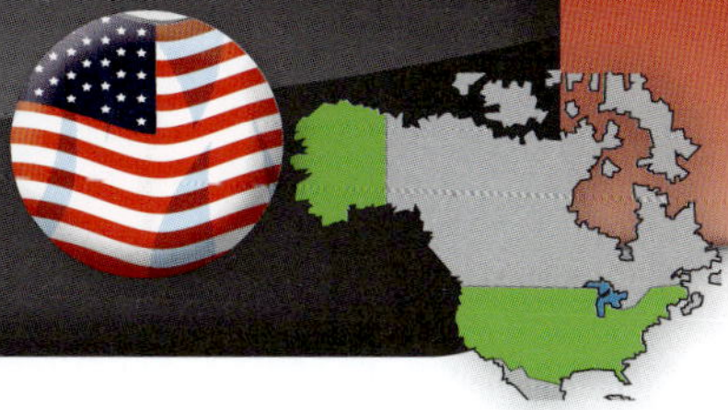

POST ✓

We have some interesting birds in the US. And bird watching is a popular activity.

Lesson 7

21 01:43 **Listen and read. Say *True* or *False*.**

1 There are only 100 different bird species in the US.

2 The National Audubon Society is an organization that protects birds in the US.

3 Many families in the US capture wild birds at their homes.

4 Some families have birdhouses in their yards.

5 The robin is one of the most common birds in US yards.

6 Laws in the US protect some bird species.

Everyday chit-chat

! How to describe what you can see

22 01:44 **Listen and repeat.**

1 
binoculars

2 
horizon

3 
hills

4 
building

23 01:45 **Listen and read. Repeat.**

Becky: Look. The view from up here is great.
Carrie: Yes, it is. What's that big white building over there?
Becky: That's the hospital. And on the right of it, you can see my school.
Carrie: Oh yes. And what's that over there, on the horizon?
Becky: Those are the hills where we went yesterday and had a picnic.
Carrie: Can I have the binoculars for a moment?
Becky: Of course. What can you see?
Carrie: Not a lot.
Becky: Because you have the binoculars the wrong way around!
Carrie: Oh yeah! You're right! Ah, that's better!

24 **Do a role play.**

CLIL
Geography

Hi there! In New Zealand there are a lot of volcanoes. At school, we learn about volcanoes in our geography class. This text is a project from my geography class. It tells you all about volcanoes.

Lesson 8

25 Listen and read. 01:46

Volcanoes

What is a volcano?

Inside the earth, there is a layer of very hot liquid rock. A volcano is a place where this hot rock can escape through a hole in the surface. When this happens, we call it a volcanic eruption. When a volcano erupts, the hot liquid rock cools down in the air and solidifies on the surface around the hole. Because of this, most volcanoes are mountains.

Types of volcano

We can put volcanoes in three categories:

1. **Active volcanoes** erupt fairly often.
2. **Dormant** or **inactive volcanoes** erupted a long time ago, but they can erupt again.
3. **Extinct volcanoes** cannot erupt again.

The tallest volcano

The tallest volcano in the world is a dormant volcano called Mauna Kea. It is on the island of Hawaii. The base of Mauna Kea is 6,000 meters below sea level. The summit is 4,205 meters above sea level. From the base to the summit, Mauna Kea is 10,205 meters tall.

The largest volcano in the solar system

The largest volcano in the solar system is on Mars. It is called Olympus Mons. It is an incredible 25 kilometers high! That's three times higher than Mount Everest!

THINKING SKILLS
Defining

26 **Read and define.** Bridge to ESO

Define these words:

1 volcano
2 magma
3 lava
4 volcanic eruption

27 **Play *Volcanic words.***

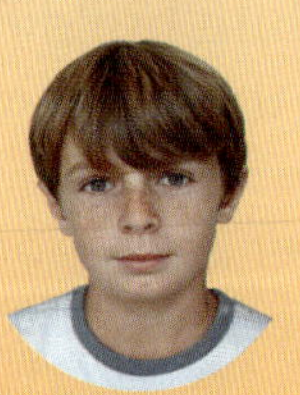

active
eruption
Hawaii

28 **Think and say.** My world

Are there any volcanoes in your country or in a country near you?

What types of volcano are they?

My words to remember
base summit volcanic rock lava eruption magma

INTERNET TRACKS Find out the name of the most active volcano in the world.

Project: Superlative quiz

29 Listen and read. 02:02

What's the widest river in the world?
a) the Amazon
b) the Nile
c) the Thames

What's the most populated country in the world?
a) India
b) the US
c) China

Yesterday at school, I made these superlative quiz cards. Can you answer the questions? POST ✓

Becky: Question number 1. What's the widest river in the world? Is it a) the Amazon, b) the Nile or c) the Mississippi?

Friend: I think the answer is the Nile.

Becky: I'm sorry. It isn't the Nile. The widest river in the world is the Amazon. The Nile is the longest.

30 Plan your project.

THINKING SKILLS
Remembering

1. Find out superlative facts about animals and geographical features.
2. Prepare your questions.
3. Think of two incorrect answers for each question.
4. Write and present your quiz.

You can also present your quiz on a computer.

Which is the smallest type of penguin in the world?

A. the blue penguin
B. the emperor penguin
C. the king penguin

AB page 22

Do the Unit 2 Review and Self-assessment (Activity Book page 22). Complete your *Progress Journal* for Unit 2.

3 Recipes and food

AIMS

In this unit:

- I **name** and **describe** different types of food.
- I **listen to** and **read** a survival story *The hurricane and the coconut tree.*
- I **ask** and **answer** questions about food.
- I **find out about** Jamaican and US culture.
- I **act out** giving instructions in the kitchen in a role play.
- I **read about** products from trees, and **write** and **present** a project.

Lesson 1

1 02:06 **Listen and say.**

Tiger Tracks SLN POST ✓

Hi there. I'm Florence from Jamaica. We have many kinds of food in my country. Which of these foods does Jamaica produce? Does your country produce the same foods?

1 coconuts

2 salt

3 coffee

4 spices

5 beans

6 citrus fruits

7 rice

8 honey

9 sugar

10 olives

2 02:07 **Listen and find out. Which foods does Jamaica produce? Now ask and talk about your country.**

Does your country produce coffee?

Yes, I think so. | I'm not really sure. | No, I don't think so.

3 02:08 **Listen and do the vocabulary quiz.**

They're orange, yellow and green. They have a lot of vitamin C.

INTERNET TRACKS Find a map of Jamaica. What is the name of the capital city? Where is it?

Lesson 2

4 Listen and read. 02:09

POST

I love learning about food and cooking. This is one of my favorite food blogs. I always find interesting information here, and simple but tasty recipes too! Do you think this cake looks good?

Jamaican coconuts

READING TIP Use a dictionary to find out the meaning of new words if they are important, e.g. *teaspoon* and *grated*.

Jamaica is a Caribbean island. Coconut trees grow very well in the country's warm, tropical climate. There are many coconut farms on the island and coconut is a popular ingredient in Jamaican cooking.

Jamaican Coconut Cake

Today's recipe is a cake full of Jamaican flavors. There's some coconut in it, but there are also two more ingredients from Jamaica: chocolate and lime. The cake is delicious and very simple to make.

Ingredients

175g of butter
100g of brown sugar
1 tablespoon of honey
3 eggs
175g of flour, with 2 teaspoons of baking powder
¼ of a teaspoon of salt
50g of coconut
The juice of a lime
50g of grated dark chocolate

Instructions

1. First, put the butter, sugar and honey into a bowl. Mix until the mixture is smooth.
2. Then, add the eggs one at a time. Mix after each egg.
3. Slowly add the flour, coconut and grated chocolate and mix well. Then add the lime juice and mix again.
4. Next, pour the mixture into a greased baking pan.
5. Last, put it in the oven and bake it for 30–35 minutes at 180°. Leave the cake to cool.

Serving Suggestion

Serve the cake with a glass of lemonade. Enjoy!

THINKING SKILLS
Explaining and sequencing

5 Answer the questions.

1. What type of climate does Jamaica have?
2. Which three ingredients from Jamaica are in the cake?
3. How many teaspoons of salt do you need?
4. How long do you bake the cake for?
5. What drink is good with the cake?

6 Play *Read and change.* Bridge to ESO

Jamaica is a Caribbean city.

Stop! It doesn't say city. It says island.

7 Think and say. TALK ABOUT IT!

I think Jamaican Coconut Cake looks delicious. I want to try it.

INTERNET TRACKS Find out the names of three more countries in the Caribbean.

Lesson 3

8 02:11 **Listen to and read the story.**

Sometimes there are hurricanes in Jamaica. Our grandparents all remember very bad hurricanes. They all have a survival story to tell us. This is one story. I hope you like it. POST ✓

THE HURRICANE AND THE COCONUT TREE

- **How strong is the hurricane?**
- **How old is the coconut tree?**

1 **Zach and his mother are on vacation in Jamaica. They are visiting their friends Alice and Jake.**

2 **One day, in Jamaica, there's an important message on the radio.**

3 **Everybody on the island prepares for the hurricane. They protect their houses and their animals. They put extra food and drink in their cupboards.**

4 **Later, the sky is very cloudy. The wind is very strong. The hurricane is near.**

9 **Read and say *True* or *False*. Correct the false sentences.**

1 Zach and his mom live in Jamaica.
2 People hear about the hurricane on the radio.
3 Alice and Jake see a girl in a car under the coconut tree.
4 The girl in the story is Zach's sister.
5 Zach's mom saved Alice and Jake's life.
6 In picture 9, the coconut tree is more than 20 years old.

Tiger Values
Think about it!

Is it important to prepare for the weather? Why?
How do you prepare for the weather in your country?

Do you know...?

We give hurricanes names. Hurricane Gilbert devastated Jamaica in 1988. It destroyed towns, farms and the countryside. Sadly, it also killed 200 people.

10 Ask and say.

TALK ABOUT IT!

1 Do you like the story? Why? / Why not?
2 What's your favorite part of the story?
3 Do you think it was a good idea to plant a tree to say thank you to Jake and Alice?
4 Do you want to visit Jamaica?

Everyday phrases: learn and use!

Try some. It's delicious!

The wind is very strong.

I don't believe it!

Please, come inside with us.

GRAMMAR TRACKS

Lesson 4

11 02:12 **Listen and read. Predict what they want to make.**

Father: **Is there any** flour in the cabinet?
Boy: Yes, there is. **There are two** packets of flour. And **there are three** boxes of sugar.
Father: **Is there any** milk in the fridge?
Girl: Yes, there is. **There are four** bottles of milk. And **there's some** butter, too.
Father: **Are there any** eggs?
Boy: Yes, there are.
Girl: **There are three**, four, five eggs.
Father: OK. We have all the ingredients we need. Let's make …

12 **Act out the dialogue.**

13 02:13 **Listen, repeat and learn.**

Countable and uncountable nouns

There	is	an egg.
	are	some eggs.

There	isn't	a bottle of milk.
	aren't	any bottles of milk.

Is	there	an apple?	Yes,	there is.	No,	there isn't.
Are		any apples?		there are.		there aren't.

Uncountable nouns

There	is	some milk.

There	isn't	any flour.

Is	there	any flour?	Yes, there is.	No, there isn't.

14 **Be a grammar detective! Look at page 27 in the AB.**

Can you count flour?
Can you count packets of flour?
Do we use *There is…* or *There are…* with uncountable nouns?

Can you find five examples of these structures in the story?
***There is(n't)* + uncountable noun**
***There are(n't)* + countable noun**

FAST TRACK GRAMMAR *Write a list of uncountable nouns that are in your school.*

Lesson 5

Sound track

15 02:14 **Listen and read. What do you notice about the words in green? Listen and repeat.**

Look! There are two chickens sitting on their legs.

They're not sitting on their legs, they're sitting on their eggs.

16 02:15 **Listen and say *True* or *False*. Correct the false sentences.**

17 **Play *Which cabinet?***

Is there any orange juice?

No, there isn't. But there are two oranges.

Are there any eggs?

Yes, there are. There are five eggs.

Are you looking at cabinet 2?

Yes, I am!

18 **Write a list of five foods in your fridge.** **Ask and answer questions.**

Do you have any milk in your fridge?

Yes, I do. I have some cheese.

No, I don't. Do you have any cheese in your fridge?

FAST TRACK GRAMMAR *Write a dialogue like the one in Activity 17 using different foods.*

In Jamaica, you can eat a lot of different kinds of international food. This article makes me want to try dishes from different countries around the world.

POST ✓

Lesson 6

19 Listen and read. 02:16

Eating out in Kingston, Jamaica

In Kingston, the capital of Jamaica, there are many different types of restaurants and cafés. They cook food from many different countries around the world. There are Spanish bars where you can try tapas and paella. There are Italian pizzerias where you can try different types of pasta and pizza. There are Japanese restaurants where you can try sushi. Or how about a curry at an Indian restaurant? Or a chilli con carne at a Mexican restaurant? They're all delicious. But if you're on vacation in Jamaica, why not try a traditional Jamaican dish? Jamaican cooking includes a lot of the ingredients that the island produces. It is often fruity and spicy.

Jamaican rice with red beans
This very popular dish is made with rice, coconut milk, onions, spices and red beans. It's delicious. Jamaicans often have it with chicken for lunch on Sunday.

Baked Jamaican bananas
In Jamaica you can eat red bananas! They are smaller and sweeter than yellow bananas. You can bake them with butter, sugar, lime juice and spices. People eat them hot with ice cream. Mmm. Delicious.

Lemonade
This cool, refreshing drink is very popular all year in Jamaica. It's made with lemons, limes, water, brown sugar and spices. A glass of lemonade with ice really is the taste of Jamaica!

What types of restaurants and cafés are there where you live?
What traditional dishes are popular in your country?

20 **Read and guess.** 02:17 **Listen and say the answers.**

POST ✓

How much do you know about Jamaica? Let's find out.

Culture quiz time: Jamaica

1. Where's the island of Jamaica? **a)** in the Mediterranean Sea **b)** in the Pacific Ocean **c)** in the Caribbean Sea
2. What's the capital of Jamaica? **a)** Kingston **b)** Queenston **c)** Princeton
3. What's the official language of Jamaica? **a)** French **b)** English **c)** Spanish
4. What type of music comes from Jamaica? **a)** jazz **b)** reggae **c)** pop
5. What foods does Jamaica produce? **a)** bananas, sugar and spices **b)** olives, pumpkins and tea **c)** milk, cheese and yogurt
6. In which sport does Jamaica have a lot of world champions? **a)** swimming **b)** soccer **c)** track and field

POST ✓

The US is famous for hamburgers, and for apple pie. It is also famous for a big American breakfast.

Lesson 7

21 02:19 **Listen and read. Say *True* or *False*.**

1 A big American breakfast includes eggs, sausages, hash browns, pancakes, toast and a large glass of orange juice or coffee.

2 In the past, it was the breakfast of farmers and workmen who needed a lot of energy.

3 Nowadays, most people have lemon juice and toast for breakfast.

4 People never have a big American breakfast on the weekend.

5 "Brunch" is a combination of the words "breakfast" and "lunch".

Everyday chit-chat

! How to give instructions in the kitchen

22 02:20 **Listen and repeat.**

1 slice of bread

2 cream cheese

3 slices of apple

4 chips

23 02:21 **Listen and read. Repeat.**

Becky: This is my favorite type of sandwich.
Carrie: What's in it?
Becky: Cream cheese, apple and chips.
Carrie: That's unusual! How do you make it?
Becky: It's really easy. First, you put some cream cheese on a slice of bread. Then you put some slices of apple on the cheese.
Carrie: Then what?
Becky: Then you put some peanuts and chips on top of the apple.
Carrie: OK. That isn't difficult. What next?
Becky: Next, you put some more apple on top of the chips. Lastly, you put another slice of bread on top of the apple and you press it down. Then you cut the sandwich in half and eat it.
Carrie: Mmmm! I don't believe it! It's delicious!

24 **Do a role play.**

CLIL

Natural Science

Lesson 8

Hi there! I love trees. They give us coconuts, bananas and spices. But there are many other things that come from trees, too. Here's a website which tells us about some of the products we get from trees.

POST ✓

25 02:22 **Listen and read.**

Generous trees

Trees give us so many things. They give us fruit, chocolate and coconuts to eat and coffee to drink. They give us wood to make houses and furniture. And did you know that natural rubber comes from a tree too? Here are some more things that come from trees.

Oxygen

There is one thing that all trees give us. You can't see it, but it's all around us. It's in the air. It's oxygen. In a process called photosynthesis, trees absorb carbon dioxide and turn it into oxygen.

Medicines

Many types of medicine come from trees. Aspirin, for example. Aspirin is a natural product that comes from the bark of willow trees. In the 18th century, people used willow bark to make a type of tea. The tea helped people who were in pain. Nowadays, aspirin is made in laboratories.

Cork

Do you have a cork bulletin board at school? Where does the cork come from? It comes from the bark of a special type of oak tree. The tree grows in Spain, Portugal and France. People take the bark off the trees. This process does not harm the tree. The bark grows back every 7 to 10 years.

Paper

The main ingredient of paper is wood fibers. Factories mix wood fibers with water and chemicals to make paper. But factories can also make new paper from old magazines and newspapers. It's important to recycle paper because it saves trees.

Chewing gum

Natural chewing gum is made from a thick liquid that comes from the sapodilla tree. People cut the tree and collect the liquid in buckets. To make natural chewing gum, they add flavoring and sugar to the liquid.

THINKING SKILLS
Deciding and justifying

26 Read and answer. Bridge to ESO

1. Write a list of twelve things which come from trees.
2. In your opinion, which three things on your list are the most important? Why?

27 Play *Search and find*. Write.

Find in the text:

- *two things you can read*
- *three parts of a tree*
- *two types of gas*
- *three countries*
- *five things you can eat*
- *two things you can drink*

28 Think and say. My world

How many trees can you name in English?

What kinds of trees are near where you live?

My words to remember

medicines cork
oxygen chewing gum
paper natural rubber

INTERNET TRACKS General Sherman is a tree in the US. Find out why it is special.

Project: A recipe

This is my favorite recipe. It's easy and delicious. Do you have all the ingredients? Do you want to make it?

POST ✓

29 02:24 **Listen and read.**

Baked apples with ice cream

Introduction

We have an apple tree in our yard so we eat a lot of apples. Baked apples with ice cream is one of my favorite desserts and it's very easy to make.

Ingredients

4 apples the same size
2 tablespoons of raisins
1 teaspoon of cinnamon
4 teaspoons of butter
2 teaspoons of brown sugar

Preparation time

15 minutes

Cooking time

25 minutes

Instructions

- First, put the raisins, the brown sugar and the cinnamon in a bowl and mix them together.
- Then, wash the apples. Cut out the center of each apple. (Be very careful. Don't cut yourself. Ask someone to help you.)
- Next, put the apples in a dish. Put the raisins, cinnamon and sugar mixture into each apple. And put a teaspoon of butter on top.
- Last, put the dish into the oven. Bake the apples at 200° for 20 to 25 minutes.

Serving suggestions

Serve your baked apples in a bowl with ice cream.

By Ed

30 Plan your project.

THINKING SKILLS
Explaining and sequencing

1. Choose a favorite dish.
2. Find out what ingredients you need.
3. Find out how to make the dish.
4. Write and present your recipe.

You can also present your project in this way.

First, put the raisins, the brown sugar and the cinnamon in a bowl and mix them together.

AB page 32

Do the Unit 3 Review and self-assessment (Activity Book page 32). Complete your *Progress Journal* for Unit 3.

4 Around the city

AIMS

In this unit:

- I **name** and **describe** places in towns and cities.
- I **listen to** and **read** a detective story *The alibi.*
- I **talk about** where people were at different times yesterday.
- I **find out about** Irish and US culture.
- I **act out** finding out about opening and closing times in a role play.
- I **read about** how people use technology, and **write** and **present** a project.

Lesson 1

1 02:28 **Listen and say.**

Tiger Tracks SLN POST

Hi everyone. My name's Finn. I live in Dublin, the capital of Ireland. I think it's a great city. Can you guess which of these things Dublin doesn't have? Do you have all these things where you live?

1 
airport

2 
botanical garden

3 
sports stadium

4 

post office

5 
port

6 

bank

7 
theme park

8 
shopping center

9 
main square

10 

tourist information office

2 02:29 **Listen and find out. Which places does Dublin not have? Now ask and talk about your town.**

Does your town have an airport?

Yes, it does. | I think so. | I don't think so. | No, it doesn't.

3 02:30 **Listen and do the vocabulary quiz.**

It's a place where you can see ships and boats.

INTERNET TRACKS Find a map of Ireland. What is the name of the capital city? Where is it?

Lesson 2

POST ✓ At the moment, a girl from Spain is staying with my family. She's learning English. Yesterday, I helped her write this letter to her friends at home. Do you think Dublin is a good city to visit?

4 Listen and read.

02:31

Dear all,

This letter is in English because I need to practice writing. Finn is helping me.

I'm having a lot of fun in Dublin. It's a great city! ☺☺ The people are friendly and my host family is fantastic, especially Finn. They have a very nice house in the city center. I can see Dublin Castle from my bedroom window. ☺

From Monday to Friday I go to school with Finn and his sister. The school isn't in the city center. It takes twenty minutes to go by bus, but there's a lot to see on the journey. Dublin is so beautiful! There are parks and museums. There are some incredible bridges over the river. There's a port. And, of course, there are a lot of shopping centers. Fantastic! I love shopping! ☺☺

Last Saturday, I was at the sports stadium for a pop concert. The music wasn't very good ☹ but the stadium was amazing! ☺

My favorite place in Dublin is the botanical garden. Wow! It's gorgeous! I love looking at all the exotic plants.

See you soon.

Best wishes,

Ana

P.S. I hope you like the photos.

READING TIP The use of smiley faces can help you understand how the writer feels.

THINKING SKILLS
Reporting

5 Correct the sentences.

1 Ana says Dublin is a horrible city.
2 Ana says she can see a park from her window.
3 Ana says she hates shopping.
4 Ana says her favorite place is the stadium.
5 Ana says she loves looking at exotic animals.

6 Play *Read and change.*

Bridge to ESO

Dear everyone.

Stop. It doesn't say everyone. It says all.

7 Think and say.

TALK ABOUT IT!

I want to stay with a family in Dublin because I like people from Ireland.

INTERNET TRACKS Find out the names of two parks in Dublin.

Lesson 3

8 Listen to and read the story. 02:33

POST

In my free time, I like writing and illustrating stories. This is one of my detective stories. I hope you enjoy it.

The alibi

- **Where does the robbery happen?**
- **How many people plan it?**

9 **Read and answer the questions.**

1 Where is the detective from?
2 Who is the woman at the airport?
3 When did the robbery happen?
4 What is special about the diamond?
5 Where do the police find the diamond?
6 How does the detective know that Olivia has an identical twin sister?

Tiger Values
Think about it!

Is it important to tell the police if you know something about a crime? Why?
How do the police help people in your community?

Do you know...?
Identical twins always have different fingerprints.

10 **Ask and say.** TALK ABOUT IT!

1 What type of story is *The alibi*?
2 Do you like the story? Why? / Why not?
3 What's your favorite part of the story?
4 Do you like writing stories?

Everyday phrases: learn and use!

My pleasure.
You were right.
Thank you for your help.
Do you know the answer?

GRAMMAR TRACKS

Lesson 4

11 02:34 **Listen and read.** **Act out the dialogues.**

Policeman: Mr Green, **where were you** at **two ten** yesterday afternoon?
Mr Green: **I was** in the museum souvenir store.
Policeman: Did you see Olivia Jones?
Mr Green: Yes, I did. She **was** in the store, talking on her cell phone. She said, "I have the diamond. Meet me at the Dragon Hotel in half an hour."

Policewoman: Mrs Brown, **where were you** yesterday afternoon?
Mrs Brown: I **was** in the Dragon Hotel.
Policewoman: Was Olivia Jones in the hotel?
Mrs Brown: Yes, she was. She **was** at the hotel reception desk at **two fifty**. She **was** with her sister.

12 **Play *Guess the time.***

13 02:35 **Listen, repeat and learn.**

***was* and *were* + *at* (place) + *at* (time)**

Where	was he / she were you / they	at	10:00 14:00 17:45	yesterday?

I / He / She / It	was	at	the park school home	at	10:00. 14:00. 17:45.
You / We / They	were				

I / He / She / It	wasn't	at	the park school home	at	10:00. 14:00. 17:45.
You / We / They	weren't				

Was he / she	at home? at the park?	Yes,	he / she was.	No,	he / she wasn't.
Were we / they			we / they were.		we / they weren't.

14 **Be a grammar detective! Look at page 37 in the AB.**

Do we use *was* and *were* to talk about the past or the future?

Is *two fifty-five* before or after three o'clock?

Is *three oh five* before or after three o'clock?

Can you find two examples of the time in the dialogue of the story?

What time is it in each picture of the story? Find the clocks.

FAST TRACK GRAMMAR *Write five sentences about where you were yesterday.*

Lesson 5

Sound track /ə/

15 02:36 **Listen and identify. Listen and repeat. Point and say.**

It's three **o'clock**.
It's eleven **o'clock**.
It's eight **o'clock**.
It's four **o'clock**.

a 
b 
c 
d 

16 02:37 **Listen and say *True* or *False*. Correct the false sentences.**

Clare			 Isabel	
Ben				
Sam	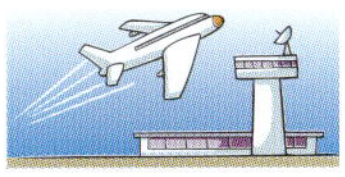	 Ben		
Isabel	 Sam			 Clare

17 **Play *Where were you?***

Where were you at nine fifty five yesterday?

I was at the airport.

Where were you at three twenty?

I was at Isabel's house.

You're Clare!

Yes, that's right!

18 **Talk about where you were yesterday or last Saturday.**

Where were you yesterday at four fifteen?

I don't remember. I think I was at a friend's house.

FAST TRACK GRAMMAR *Write five sentences about where your friends were yesterday.*

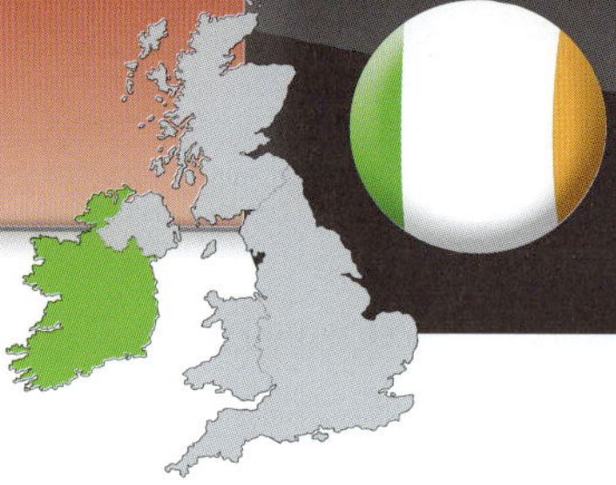

Cult

In Ireland, there are a lot of traditional songs which most people know. This article is about one of our most famous songs.

POST ✓

Lesson 6

19 02:39 **Listen and read.**

Molly Malone

The statue of Molly Malone in Dublin is famous. But who is Molly Malone?

Molly Malone is a character from a traditional song. Almost everyone in Ireland knows the song. Almost everyone in Ireland can sing it. And there are many professional recordings of the song. It is possibly one of the most famous and popular songs in the country.

The song tells Molly's story. She is a beautiful girl who sells fresh seafood in Dublin. She doesn't work in a store. She sells the seafood from a wheelbarrow.

In Dublin's fair city,
Where the girls are so pretty,
I first set my eyes on sweet Molly Malone,
As she wheeled her wheelbarrow,
Through streets broad and narrow,
Crying "Cockles and mussels, alive, alive, oh!"
"Alive, alive, oh,
Alive, alive, oh",
Crying "Cockles and mussels, alive, alive, oh".

A cockle

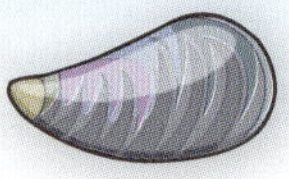

A mussel

Later in the song, Molly dies of a fever. People miss her, but they believe that her ghost continues to walk in the streets of Dublin, crying *Cockles and mussels, alive, alive, oh!*

Who are the most famous characters from books or songs in your country?

Are there any traditional songs in your country which everyone knows?

20 **Read and guess.** 02:41 **Listen and say the answers.**

POST ✓

Are you ready for a culture quiz on Ireland? Good luck!

Culture quiz time: Ireland

1. What's the capital of Ireland? **a)** Cardiff **b)** Edinburgh **c)** Dublin
2. What are the colors of the Irish flag? **a)** red, white and green **b)** red, white and blue **c)** green, white and orange
3. Who is the patron saint of Ireland? **a)** St George **b)** St David **c)** St Patrick
4. Which musical instrument is a symbol of Ireland? **a)** a guitar **b)** a harp **c)** a drum
5. What's the most common surname in Ireland? **a)** Murphy **b)** Smith **c)** Jones
6. What type of animal doesn't live in Ireland? **a)** snakes **b)** mosquitoes **c)** pigeons

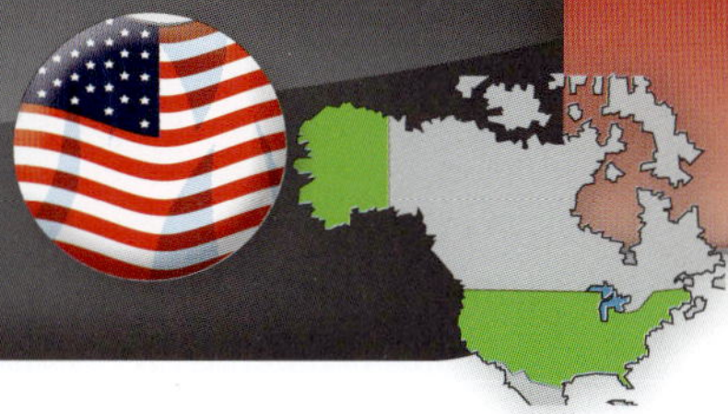

In the US, most statues are of real people from history. But some statues are of very famous characters from literature, like Rip Van Winkle.

POST ✓

Lesson 7

21 02:43 **Listen and read. Say *True* or *False*.**

1. Rip Van Winkle is a character from American literature.
2. Rip Van Winkle lives in a small town near the Catskill Mountains in Vermont.
3. The story of Rip Van Winkle was published in 1919.
4. The story of Rip Van Winkle was written by American author Washington Irving.
5. Rip Van Winkle is set in the years before and after the American Revolutionary War.
6. The Rip Van Winkle statue is in Irvington, New York.

Everyday chit-chat

! How to find out about opening and closing times

22 03:01 **Listen and repeat.**

1 
information

2 
wheelchair access

3 
elevator

4 
restaurant

23 03:02 **Listen and read. Repeat.**

Woman: Good morning. This is the Tourist Information Office. How can I help you?
Becky: Hello. Can you tell me what time the Science Museum opens on Saturdays, please?
Woman: It opens at 10 o'clock in the morning. It closes at 6 o'clock in the evening.
Becky: Does it close for lunch?
Woman: No, it's open all day. And there are cafés and restaurants in the museum.
Becky: Are there any special exhibitions this month?
Woman: Yes. There's an exhibition about robots. You can find information about it on the museum website.
Becky: One last question. Is there wheelchair access?
Woman: Yes, there is. The wheelchair access is very good and there are elevators to every floor.
Becky: Thank you very much.
Woman: You're welcome.

24 **Do a role play.**

Lesson 8

I'm not very techy but I use a computer program to create my comic strips. This article is about how other people from Dublin use technology. POST ✓

25 03:03 **Listen and read.**

TECHNOLOGY in the city

Technology plays an important part in our lives today. Five people from Dublin tell us how they use technology in the city.

1. GPS

I'm a taxi driver in Dublin. I have GPS in the taxi. I use it to find addresses in the city. It also tells me if there are any traffic problems. GPS technology makes my job a lot easier.

2. TABLETS

We use a tablet to go online. We look up the opening times of stores and museums. We also find out what's showing at the movie theater and what time the movies start. It's easier, cheaper and quicker than a phone call.

3. WIFI ZONES & LAPTOPS

I'm lucky. I have a small laptop. I use it to send emails and to chat to my friends. I can now do those things in the city center because there are a lot of places with free wifi zones: cafés, the library, parks, etc. I like using my laptop in the park. I can do my homework and get fresh air at the same time!

4. APPS & SMARTPHONES

I'm learning French. I don't have much time to practice. But now I'm learning words and expressions with an app on my smartphone. It's great because I can use it anywhere in the city.

5. ONLINE SHOPPING

I love online shopping. I send my shopping list to the supermarket and they deliver everything to my house. It's so easy and it saves me a lot of time.

CAN YOU IMAGINE YOUR LIFE WITHOUT TECHNOLOGY?

THINKING SKILLS
Paraphrasing

Bridge to ESO

26 **Read and complete the sentences.**

1 He likes using GPS because it…
2 They use a tablet to…
3 He uses wifi zones and his laptop to…
4 She uses an app on her smartphone to…
5 She does online shopping because it…

27 **Play *Five reasons why.***

28 **Think and say.**

My world

How does technology affect your life?
Which electronic gadgets do you use at home and at school?

My words to remember
wifi zone online shopping app go online chat smartphone

INTERNET TRACKS These words are abbreviations: *www*, *GPS*, *app*. Find out what they stand for.

Project: A guide for tourists

29 03:05 **Listen and read.**

Read my project about Orlando. What can you see from the top of the Orlando Eye? What time does Lake Kissimmee State Park close? POST ✓

Places to visit in

Orlando

Orlando is a city in central Florida. I was there last August. Here are two places I can recommend.

The Orlando Eye is a very popular tourist attraction in Orlando. It's 122 meters tall. I recommend the eye because you can see incredible views of the city. From the top of the eye you can see parks, lakes and attractions from the theme park. You can see Big Sand Lake and Little Sand Lake. On a clear day, you can see the Kennedy Space Center. The eye turns 360° and the ride lasts about 30 minutes. Check online for ticket prices and opening times. The eye has wheelchair access.

Lake Kissimmee State Park is one of Orlando's largest lakes. I recommend the park because it's the perfect place for a quiet walk or a bike ride. There are campsites in the park. There's a lake where you can rent a boat. For sporty people, there are areas where you can play volleyball, soccer and other sports. If you want to take your laptop, there is a marina and camp store with wifi zones. The park closes at sundown.

By Becky

30 **Plan your project.**

THINKING SKILLS
Explaining

1. Choose a town or city you know.
2. Find out about places to visit.
3. Find out about the opening times.
4. Write and present your recommendations.

You can also present your project in this way.

→ AB page 42

Do the Unit 4 Review and Self-assessment (Activity Book page 42). Complete your *Progress Journal* for Unit 4.

5 Ingenious inventions

AIMS

In this unit:

- I **name** and **talk about** inventions.
- I **listen to** and **read** a true story *The discovery of vaccination.*
- I **ask** and **answer** questions about people's lives in the past.
- I **find out about** English and US culture.
- I **act out** talking about what I did at school in a role play.
- I **read about** the history of an invention, and **write** and **present** a project.

Lesson 1

1 03:07 **Listen and say.**

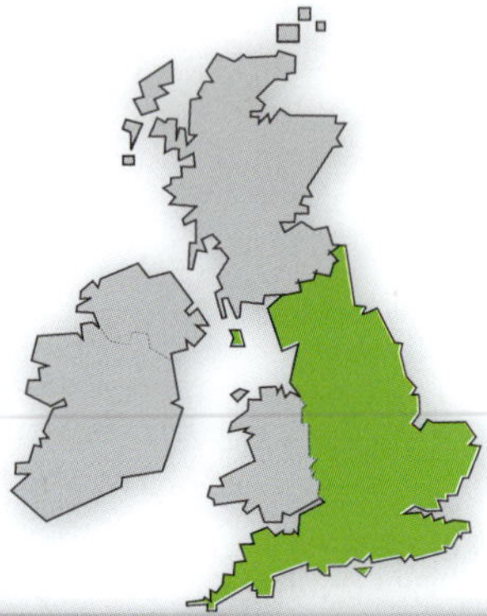

Tiger Tracks SLN POST ✓

Hi. I'm Kim. I live in Manchester, in England. My favorite subjects at school are history and science. I'm especially interested in the history of things we use every day. One of these inventions is from England. Do you know which one? Do you know how old these inventions are?

1 
light bulb

2 
stamps

3 
umbrella

4 
dishwasher

5 
Band-Aids

6 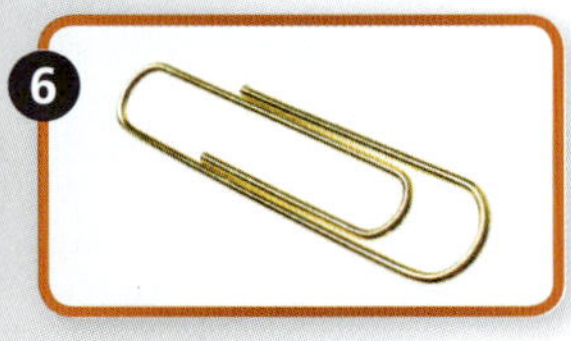
paper clip

7 
microwave

8 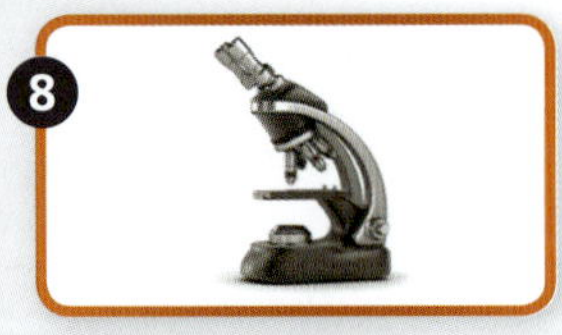
microscope

9 
bilingual dictionary

10 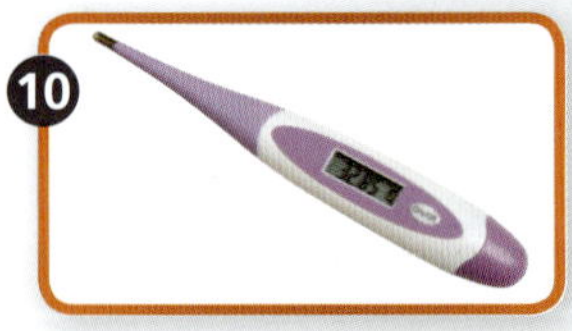
digital thermometer

2 **Discuss with a partner. Write your ideas.** 03:08 **Now listen and find out.**

How old is the light bulb?

It's more than 200 years old.

It's between 100 and 200 years old.

It's less than 100 years old.

3 03:09 **Listen and do the vocabulary quiz.** ?

You use this when you learn a foreign language.

INTERNET TRACKS Find out the name of the first stamp in the world.

Lesson 2

4 Listen and read. 03:11

I love finding out about great scientists and inventors from history. Here are four mini-biographies about four of my favorite inventors. Which do you think is the most interesting? POST

READING TIP Use the pictures to help you understand the text.

Four Inventors

Leonardo da Vinci (1452 – 1519)

Leonardo da Vinci painted the Mona Lisa, which is perhaps the most famous painting in the world. But Leonardo was also a scientist and an inventor. He invented some musical instruments and a type of clock. He also designed this flying machine.

Josephine Cochrane (1839 – 1913)

In about 1880, Josephine Cochrane had an idea. She wanted to design a machine to wash dishes. So she studied science and mechanics. She learned how to draw. She worked on her design for six years. Finally, in 1886, her dishwashing machine was complete.

Thomas Edison (1847 – 1931)

Thomas Edison invented many things. He invented the phonograph (a machine for recording sound), a type of battery and a type of car. But his most famous invention was a type of light bulb. He was not the first person to invent a light bulb, but his design was the most efficient. Nowadays, there are light bulbs for bicycles, cell phones, fridges and microscopes. Can you imagine life without light bulbs?

George Lerner (1922 – 1995)

In 1949, George Lerner invented a plastic toy called Mr Potato Head. At first, the toy was not a success. But in 1952, Mr Potato Head appeared in a television commercial. Then every child wanted the toy. Today, Mr Potato Head is one of the most popular toys in the world. He is also a character in the *Toy Story* movies.

THINKING SKILLS
Sequencing

5 Put these events in chronological order.

- Leonardo da Vinci painted the Mona Lisa.
- Mr Potato Head appeared on television.
- Thomas Edison died.
- Josephine Cochrane invented the first dishwasher.

6 Play a memory game.

Who invented a type of clock?

Leonardo da Vinci.

Yes, that's right!

7 Think and say.

TALK ABOUT IT!

I think two of the greatest inventions are the cell phone and the car.

INTERNET TRACKS Think of an object you use every day. Try to find out who invented it.

Lesson 3

8 Listen to and read the story.

POST ✓ This is a true story about one of my favorite scientists. It's the story of one of the most important discoveries in history. I hope you like it.

The discovery of vaccination

- What was smallpox?
- What did Edward Jenner discover?

In the 18th century, a terrible disease called smallpox killed 10% of the population every year. It killed men, women and children. It killed rich people and poor people. It killed kings and queens.

9 **Read and say *True* or *False*. Correct the false sentences.**

1 Edward Jenner was a doctor in a large city.
2 Sarah worked on a farm with horses.
3 Cowpox can't kill you.
4 The boy didn't get cowpox.
5 The Latin word for cow is vaccination.
6 Cowpox is more serious than smallpox.

Tiger Values
Think about it!

Is it important to prevent illness and disease? Why?
What do you do to prevent illness?

Do you know...?
The last case of smallpox was in 1977.

10

Doctors continued to use and develop Jenner's vaccination theories. Today there aren't any cases of smallpox in the world, and vaccination is used against many other diseases.

10 Ask and say.

TALK ABOUT IT!

1 Do you like the story? Why? / Why not?
2 What's your favorite part of the story?
3 Do you think Jenner was a good doctor?
4 Do you think Sarah and the boy were brave?

Everyday phrases: learn and use!

What's the matter?
Don't worry.
It isn't serious.
I'm feeling better.

GRAMMAR TRACKS

Lesson 4

11 03:14 **Listen and read.**

What do we know about Edward Jenner?

We know that Edward Jenner was a brilliant doctor and scientist. He developed a treatment to protect patients from smallpox. He saved the lives of many people. But **where did he live? What did he do** in his free time? **Did he have** a family? **When did he die?**

Edward Jenner lived from 1749 to 1823. He lived with his wife and three children in a small town in England called Berkeley. He often treated people at his home, but he didn't take any money from poor people.

Jenner had many hobbies. He was very interested in wildlife. In his free time, he liked watching birds and hedgehogs.

Jenner was also interested in hot air balloons, because they were a very new invention. In 1784, more than 100 years before the invention of the plane, Jenner traveled nearly 40 kilometers in a balloon.

Today, Edward Jenner's home is a museum about his life and interests.

12 **Play *Read and change.*** Bridge to ESO

Edward Jenner was a brilliant farmer.

Stop. It doesn't say farmer. It says doctor.

13 03:15 **Listen, repeat and learn.**

***Wh-* questions in the past**

Did	you / he / they	live in England? discover vaccination? have a family?	Yes,	you / he / they did.	No,	you / he / they didn't.

Where What When	did	you / he / they	live? do? die?

14 **Be a grammar detective! Look at page 47 in the AB.**

What are the short answers to questions beginning with *Did you…?*

How many *Wh-* question words do you know?

Can you find an example of a *Wh-* question in the past in the story?

FAST TRACK GRAMMAR *Write five* Wh- *questions about a famous inventor.*

Lesson 5

Sound track

15 Listen and identify the differences. Listen and repeat. 03:17

I live at home.	I live**d** at home.
I work at school.	I work**ed** at school.
I play on the weekend.	I play**ed** on the weekend.
I want to travel around the world.	I want**ed** to travel around the world.
I invent machines.	I invent**ed** machines.

16 Listen and answer the questions. 03:18

Earle Dickson
1892 – 1961
Place: US
Profession: inventor
Invention: Band-Aids

Marie Curie
1876 – 1934
Place: France
Profession: scientist
Discovery: an element called radium

Walter Frederick Morrison
1920 – 2010
Place: US
Profession: inventor
Invention: the Frisbee

17 Do three role plays.

What's your name?
My name is Earle Dickson.
When did you live?
I lived from 1892 to 1961.
Where did you live?
I lived in the US.
What did you do?
I was an inventor. I invented Band-Aids.

18 Act out one of the role plays for your friends.

FAST TRACK GRAMMAR *Write a dialogue about Marie Curie. Use* What, When *and* Where.

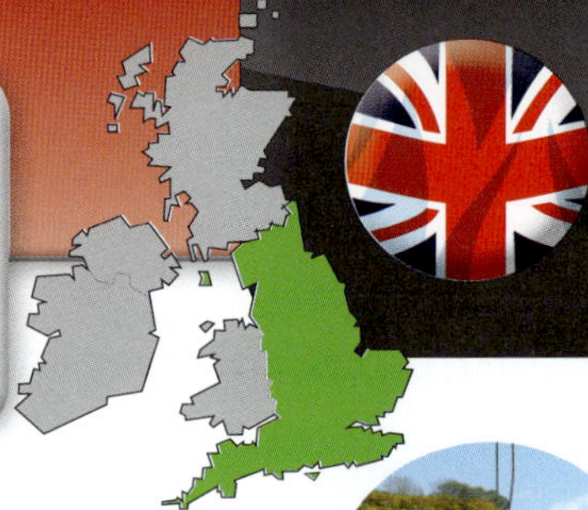

Cult

POST ✓

One of my favorite places to visit is in Cornwall, in the south west of England. It's called the Eden Project. It's a great place to learn about natural science.

Lesson 6

19 03:20 **Listen and read.**

The Eden Project

An amazing place to visit

These buildings are called biomes. Inside, you can see trees and plants that normally grow in other countries. In the Mediterranean biome you can see lemon, orange and olive trees. In the Rainforest biome there are waterfalls, and you can see banana, cacao, and chewing gum trees. If you're observant, you can also see tree frogs, butterflies, lizards and birds.

The Eden Project isn't just a garden. It teaches people about plants. There are information sheets that explain why many of the plants are important. The Eden Project gardeners also give lessons on gardening. They can teach you how to grow vegetables at home.

There are many other reasons to go to the Eden Project. There's an ice rink in winter, there's a rock climbing club, and there are beautiful sculptures in the gardens. And if you like adventure sports, you can go on the longest zip line in England!

For more information on the Eden Project, why don't you visit the Eden Project website?

Is there a place like the Eden Project in your country?

What's your favorite place to visit?

20 **Read and guess.** 03:21 **Listen and say the answers.**

POST ✓

How much do you know about England? Are you ready for the culture quiz?

Culture quiz time: England

1. Who is the patron saint of England? **a)** St Patrick **b)** St David **c)** St George
2. Which river runs through the capital city of England? **a)** the Severn **b)** the Thames **c)** the Mersey
3. Which English actor plays Harry Potter in the movies? **a)** Daniel Craig **b)** Daniel Radcliffe **c)** Rupert Grint
4. Man United is a soccer team in which city? **a)** Oxford **b)** Liverpool **c)** Manchester
5. Where does the Queen of England live? **a)** Westminster Abbey **b)** Buckingham Palace **c)** The Tower of London
6. What sport do they play at Wimbledon? **a)** cricket **b)** tennis **c)** rollerskating

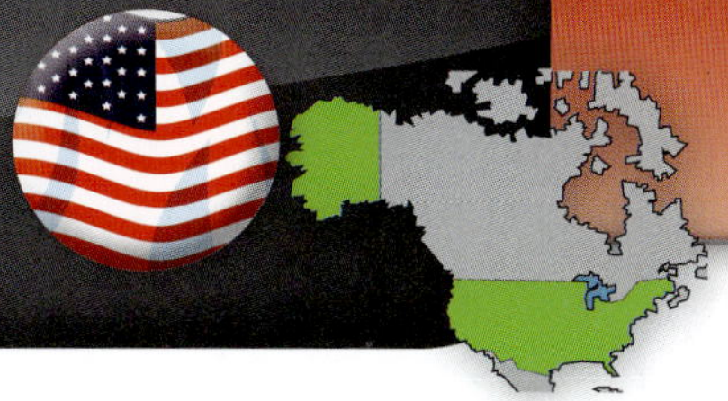

Do you like doing science projects at school? In the US there is a national competition for the best science project. POST

Lesson 7

21 **Listen and read. Say *True* or *False*.** 03:23

1 The Siemens Science Competition is every year.
2 The competition is for young people between 11 and 21 years old.
3 You can't enter a math project in the competition.
4 You can enter the competition as a team or as an individual.
5 The competition takes place all over the US, and the final is in Washington D.C.
6 The winning projects receive a prize.

Everyday chit-chat

! How to talk about what you did at school

22 **Listen and repeat.** 03:24

1 

the 19th century

2 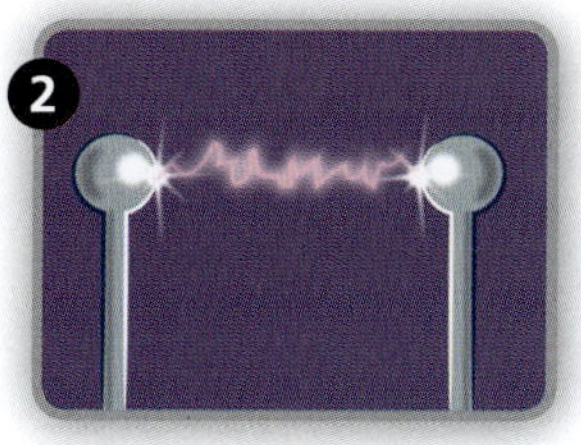
electricity

3 
batteries

4 
an idea

23 **Listen and read. Repeat.** 03:25

Dad: What did you do at school today?
Becky: A lot of things. Art, math, science and Spanish. And we started a history project.
Dad: A project! What's it about?
Becky: It's about the invention of machines in the 19th century. It's really interesting. I like history.
Dad: What did you learn in science?
Becky: Something about batteries and electricity. I didn't really understand it. It was very complicated.
Dad: Well, why don't we go to the Science Museum on the weekend? The museum always explains things simply.
Becky: That's a great idea. Can I ask a friend to come with us?
Dad: Of course.

24 **Do a role play.**

CLIL
History

Lesson 8

25 03:26 **Listen and read.**

POST ✓
Hi there! I think television is an amazing invention. This timeline shows the development of television in the US.

The history of television in the US

At the beginning of the 20th century television didn't exist. In the evenings, people talked and played games. They looked at books. Some people played musical instruments. After 1920, some people listened to the radio. Life was very different.

In 1927, an American engineer named Philo Farnsworth invented the electronic television. He transmitted the first live human images using his television system in 1929.

In the 1930s television programming was rare. Some programs were only on during weekends and some nights there were no programs at all. But most people didn't have a television at home. Television wasn't popular. People preferred the radio.

In 1950s more people began to buy televisions. By the mid-1950s television established itself as America's favorite type of entertainment.

In 1967, for the first time, some television programs were in color.

In 2000, 82% of homes in the US had more than one television.

1900 — 2000

Today, in the 21st century, televisions are bigger and better than in the past. They have flat screens and the image is very clear. There are many different channels and many different types of programs to watch. We can also watch television programs on our computers, tablets and smartphones. Some people think we now watch too much television. What do you think?

THINKING SKILLS
Sequencing

Bridge to ESO

26 **Put the events in chronological order.**

- Some programs were in color for the first time.
- Television became America's favorite type of entertainment.
- 82% of houses had two televisions.
- Televisions didn't exist.
- Some nights there were no programs at all.
- An American engineer invented the electronic television system.

27 **Play *True or False?***

Philo Farnsworth was English.

False. He was American.

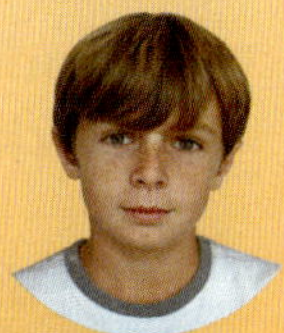

28 **Think and say.**

Is television important to you? Why? How much time do you spend watching television?

My world

My words to remember

image flat screen clear
television programs channels
at the beginning of the 20th century

INTERNET TRACKS Find out about Philo Farnsworth. When and where did he live?

Project: Inventions

29 Listen and read. 03:28

Last week at school, we did a project about inventions. I wrote this timeline about the invention of the train. How old is the train? POST

Trains

At the beginning of the 19th century, trains didn't exist. People traveled by horse and cart. They needed more than a day to travel 150 kilometers.

In 1814, an English engineer called George Stephenson invented a locomotive. It pulled 30 tons of coal up a hill. It traveled at six kilometers an hour. It was the best locomotive of the time.

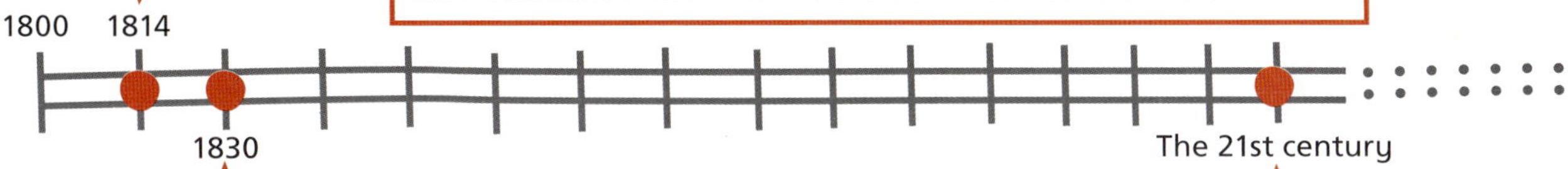

George Stephenson also designed the first train line for passengers. The line opened in September 1830. It transported people from Manchester to Liverpool. George and his son, Robert Stephenson, designed a famous locomotive for the line. It was called Stephenson's Rocket. You can see it in the Science Museum in London.

Stephenson's Rocket

Today, in the 21st century, trains are longer, faster and more comfortable than in the past. There are high-speed trains that travel at more than 400 kilometers an hour. 400 kilometers an hour! That's very fast!

A high-speed train

I think the train is a great invention. Trains save us a lot of time. We can travel to other cities and countries by train. And trains are more ecological than cars. Can you imagine life without trains?

by Ed

30 Plan your project.

THINKING SKILLS
Contrasting

1. Think of an invention. Find out who invented it and when.
2. Think about life before and after the invention. What did people do before the invention? Do people use the invention today? How?
3. Do you think it is a great invention? Why? Why not?
4. Write and present your project.

You can also present your project in this way.

AB page 52

Do the Unit 5 Review and Self-assessment (Activity Book page 52). Complete your *Progress Journal* for Unit 5.

6 Helping people

AIMS

In this unit:

- I **name** and **talk about** chores.
- I **listen to** and **read** a modern fairy tale *The red running shoes.*
- I **ask** and **answer** questions about what I did and didn't do in the past.
- I **find out about** Canadian and US culture.
- I **act out** asking for and giving directions in a role play.
- I **read about** children who help other people, and **write** and **present** a project.

Lesson 1

1 03:30 **Listen and say.**

Tiger Tracks SLN POST ✓

Hi. My name's Zoe. I live in Toronto, in Canada. At home, everyone in my family helps to do the housework. Which of these chores do you think I do? Who does these chores in your home?

1 do the dishes

2 put your clothes away

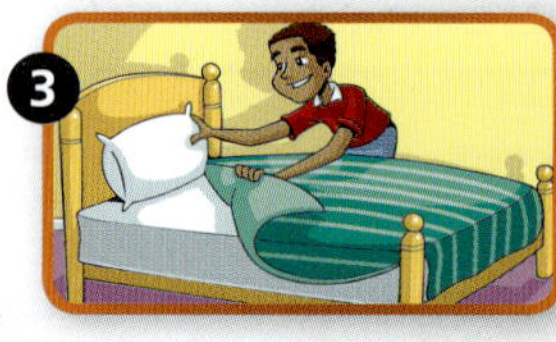

3 make your bed

4 clean up

5 clean the windows

6 take out the trash

7 feed the pets

8 water the plants

9 sweep the floor

10 wash the car

2 03:31 **Listen and find out. Which chores does Zoe do? Now ask and talk about you.**

Who makes your bed?

I usually do.

My mother / father / brother / sister does.

3 03:32 **Listen and do the vocabulary quiz. Say the missing words**

Everyone helps to ___ up in my house. We do it together.

INTERNET TRACKS Find a map of Canada. Is it bigger or smaller than the US?

Lesson 2

4 Listen and read. 03:33

My mother is an ice hockey champion. She needs to train and practice for many hours every day. My dad, my brother and I help do the chores. This is a typical day for my family. Is it similar in your family?

Life in my family

From Monday to Friday, my mother gets up at six fifteen in the morning. She has a banana and some fruit juice and then she runs 10 kilometers. I get up at seven fifteen with my dad and my little brother. I take a shower and get dressed. And then the whole family has breakfast together at seven thirty.

When my brother and I go to school, my mother goes to work. She has a part-time job in a laboratory. In the afternoon, she goes to a sports center with an ice rink. At the sports center she meets the other members of the ice hockey team. Sometimes they work with a professional trainer in the gym, and sometimes they work with their coach on the ice.

After school, my brother and I usually do some chores. We clean up. I take out the trash. My brother feeds the cat and waters the plants. Our dad does the cooking. He likes cooking. He always prepares tasty food that is good for us. When my mom comes home at six o'clock, the house is clean and dinner is ready. We always have dinner together, and we talk about what we did at school.

Last weekend, my mother played an important game. Her team didn't win, but she scored a lot of goals. I took this photo! My brother and I are very proud of our mother.

READING TIP You don't need to read every word to find the information you want.

5 Answer the questions.

1 Who waters the plants?
2 Who takes out the trash?
3 Who prepares the food?
4 Who works in a laboratory?
5 Who comes home at six o'clock?

6 Play a memory game.

THINKING SKILLS Remembering

7 Think and say.

At home, I do the dishes and I sweep the floor. I don't really like doing chores, but I think it's important to help.

INTERNET TRACKS Find out how many people are in an ice hockey team.

Lesson 3

8 Listen to and read the story. 03:35

POST
When I was younger, I liked traditional fairy tales. Now I'm older, I prefer modern fairy tales. This one is set in Canada. Enjoy! ☺

The red running shoes

- What traditional fairy tale is this similar to?
- Two people help Josh. Who?

9 **Read and answer the questions.**

1. Where did Josh live?
2. Were his stepsisters kind to Josh?
3. What did the fairy godfather give Josh?
4. Who did the dishes on the day of the marathon?
5. Was Josh the fastest runner in the marathon?
6. What is Josh doing now?

Tiger Values
Think about it!

Is it important to share housework? Why?
Do you and your family share the chores?

6 Josh joined the other runners on the starting line.

And the fairy godfather did the dishes, made the beds and took out the trash.

7 Josh was the first runner to finish the marathon.

8 Josh didn't want his stepsisters and the photographers to see him. He ran home.

9 One week later, the track and field coach visited Josh's house. He put the running shoe on Josh's foot.

10 Now, Josh is training for the next Olympics. And his stepsisters do their own cleaning.

Do you know...?
A marathon is 42.195 kilometers long. The fastest marathon runners can complete the race in less than two and a half hours!

TALK ABOUT IT!

10 Ask and say.

1 Do you like the story? Why? / Why not?
2 What's your favorite part of the story?
3 Does the story have a happy ending?
4 Do you know any other modern fairy stories?

Everyday phrases: learn and use!

Don't be sad.
I am here to help you.
Don't forget to do the dishes.
Be home before 12 o'clock.

GRAMMAR TRACKS

Lesson 4

11 03:36 **Listen to and read the poem.**

A visit from the Queen

Yesterday morning I **did** some chores.
I **made** the beds and I **swept** the floors.
I wanted the house to be very clean
For a visit from Her Majesty the Queen.

I **took** out the trash in the afternoon.
I **put** things away and I cleaned my room.
I wanted the house to be very clean
For a visit from Her Majesty the Queen.

But when the Queen arrived for tea,
At exactly three fifteen,
I didn't hear her knock at the door.
You see, I **was** exhausted from too many chores.
I **was** asleep in my rocking chair
And Her Majesty the Queen **thought** I wasn't there.

12 **Work in groups. Play *Team reading race*.**

Yesterday morning I did some chores.

I made the beds and I swept the floors.

13 03:37 **Listen, repeat and learn. Irregular verbs in the past**

Every day

I / You / We / They	take out the trash. feed the dog.
He / She	does the dishes.

Yesterday

I / You / We / They	took out the trash. fed the dog.
He / She	did the dishes.

I / You / We / They	don't	take out the trash. feed the dog.
He / She	doesn't	do the dishes.

I / You / We / They	didn't	take out the trash. feed the dog.
He / She		do the dishes.

Did	you / he / they	feed the dog? sweep the floor?	Yes,	I / you / he / they did.	No,	I / you / he / they didn't.

14 **Be a grammar detective! Look at page 57 in the AB.**

Can you remember how to form a **regular** verb in the past?

Is there a rule to help you form **irregular** verbs in the past?

How many regular and irregular verbs can you find in the story?

FAST TRACK GRAMMAR *Start an irregular verb list in your notebook.*

Lesson 5

Sound track

15 Guess the end of the sentences. Listen and check. Listen and repeat.
03:39

She didn't clean the windows, …

I didn't finish my geography test, …

She didn't win, …

… but she scored a goal.

… but she swept the floors.

… but I got a good grade.

16 Listen and say *True* or *False*. Correct the false sentences.
03:40

	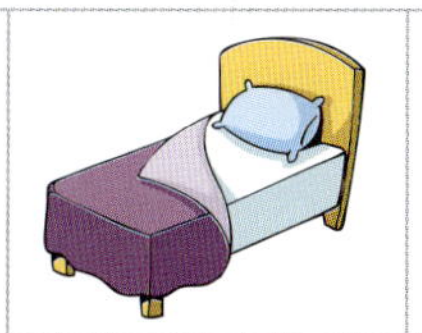					
Ruth	✓	✗	✗	✓	✗	✓
Daniel	✗	✓	✓	✗	✓	✗
Emma	✓	✓	✗	✗	✓	✗
Duncan	✗	✗	✓	✓	✗	✓

17 Play *Who am I?*

Did you take out the trash yesterday?

Yes, I did. And I made my bed.

Did you do the dishes?

No, I didn't. But I fed the dog.

You're Emma!

Yes, that's right!

18 Ask and say what you did yesterday.

Did you do any chores yesterday?

Yes, I did. I put my clothes away.

FAST TRACK GRAMMAR *Write five sentences about what you did and didn't do yesterday.*

Sports are an important part of Canadian culture. Winter sports are especially popular. And almost everyone in Canada loves watching the Winter Olympics. POST ✓

Cult

Lesson 6

19 03:42 **Listen and read.**

Canada at the Winter Olympics

The Winter Olympics take place once every four years. Sports at the Winter Olympics include skiing, skating, ice hockey and snowboarding. These are sports that need ice and snow.

Canadians are passionate about ice hockey. It's their national winter sport. Skiing and skating are also very popular in Canada. So Canadians are always very interested in the Winter Olympics. The country usually does very well.

In 2010, the Winter Olympics were in Vancouver, on the west coast of Canada. The Canadians won 14 gold medals, and the women's ice hockey team and the men's ice hockey team both won gold medals!

Tessa Virtue and Scott Moir were the ice dance Champions at the 2010 Winter Olympics. They were the youngest people to win an Olympic gold medal in the history of their sport!

Are there any famous athletes in your country? What sports are popular in your country?

20 **Read and guess.** 03:43 **Listen and say the answers.**

How much do you know about Canada? Are you ready for the culture quiz? POST ✓

Culture quiz time: Canada

1. What's the capital of Canada? **a)** Ottawa **b)** Toronto **c)** Montreal
2. What's the largest city in Canada? **a)** Ottawa **b)** Toronto **c)** Montreal
3. What can you see on the flag of Canada? **a)** a red bird **b)** a red flower **c)** a red leaf
4. Which language isn't an official language of Canada? **a)** English **b)** French **c)** Spanish
5. Which famous waterfalls are in Canada? **a)** Victoria Falls **b)** Niagara Falls **c)** Angel Falls
6. Canada is the second largest country in the world. How big is it? **a)** about 13 million km^2 **b)** about 10 million km^2 **c)** about 6 million km^2

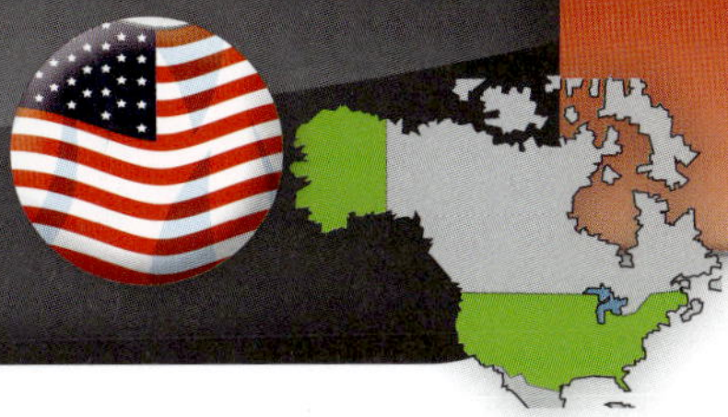

The 1996 Summer Olympics were in Altanta, Georgia. They were incredible. I love watching videos of all the different sports. POST✓

Lesson 7

21 03:45 **Listen and read. Say *True* or *False*.**

1 The Centennial Olympic Stadium is in Savannah, Georgia.
2 The 1996 Olympic Games used stadiums and an aquatics center.
3 Exactly 20 countries participated in the games.
4 More than 10,000 athletes participated in the games.
5 The American team won 4 medals. They won 2 golds, 1 silver, and 1 bronze.
6 The US post office printed stamps for the Olympics.

Everyday chit-chat

! How to ask for and give directions

22 03:46 **Listen and repeat.**

1 
turn left at the traffic lights

2 
turn right at the mailbox

3 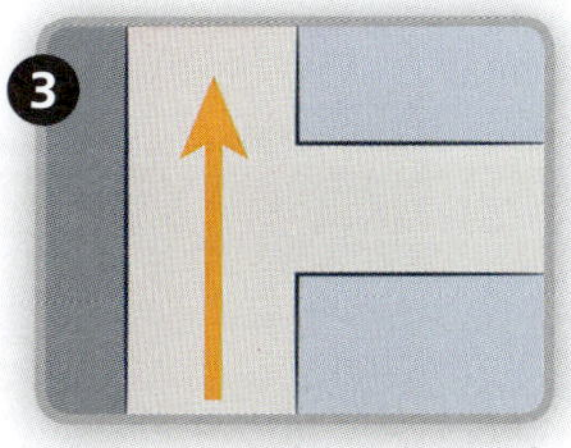
go straight ahead

4 
go under the bridge

23 03:47 **Listen and read. Repeat.**

Becky: Hello. You look lost. Can I help you?
Woman: Do you know the way to the sports stadium?
Becky: Yes. It's very close to here. Go straight ahead and turn left at the traffic light.
Woman: Left at the traffic light.
Becky: Then go straight ahead and go under the bridge.
Woman: Under the bridge.
Becky: After the bridge, turn right at the mailbox.
Woman: Right at the mailbox.
Becky: And then the sports stadium is on your left. OK?
Woman: I'm sorry. I'm French and my English is not very good. Can you repeat it?
Becky: I can show you the way. It isn't far.
Woman: Oh. OK. That's very kind of you. Thank you.
Becky: It's this way.

24 **Do a role play.**

Lesson 8

25 Listen and read. 04:01

I'm very sporty. Every Saturday I work as volunteer at a sports club for young children. I help the adults watch the children. It's fun. This webpage explains how teenagers around the world help other people. POST

Children and teenagers in action

All around the world, children and teenagers are helping to make their communities better places. They give up their free time to help neighbors and charity organizations. Their actions improve many people's lives.

Help an elderly neighbor

This is Gemma. She lives with her family in Michigan in the US. Their neighbor, Molly, is 86 years old. Gemma visits Molly every day and offers help. She sweeps her sidewalk and waters her plants. And she talks to Molly about her life at school.

Nature clean-up

Nick and his friends help to clean up nature in the US. They meet on the weekend once a month. They go to rivers, beaches, parks and forests to pick up all the litter they can find. Sometimes they have competitions to see who can find the most litter.

Walk dogs

Leroy and his younger sister are volunteer dog walkers. Every weekend they go to a charity organization for abandoned dogs in Dublin. They take the dogs for walks in the park. They also help to train the dogs.

Visit a retirement home

Lisa's favorite subject is technology class. She's good with computers. So, once a week she visits a retirement home in Wellington. She teaches the elderly how to send emails and how to use a social network. With Lisa's help, some of the elderly are writing blogs.

Can you do more to help people in your community?

THINKING SKILLS
Analysing

Bridge to ESO

26 Read, think and answer.

What is a good way to help people in your community…
…if you're very techy?
…if you like walking?
…if you like nature?
…if you like chatting to people?
…if you like animals?

27 Play *Question challenge*.

Where does Gemma live?

In the US. How does she help?

She visits an elderly neighbor called Molly. How often does she visit Molly?

Every day.

28 Think and say.

Do you help people in your community?
Can you think of new ways to help people in your community?

My world

My words to remember

retirement home · charity · pick up litter
elderly neighbor · walk the dog · elderly

INTERNET TRACKS Research these charities: SPCA, Habitat for Humanity and the United Way. What do they do?

Project: How we can help

29 04:03 **Listen and read.**

This is a project we did at school. Do you like my ideas for helping? POST

How I help people at home

I live with my mother and father, my little brother and our dog, Buster. At home I often help my parents do the chores. I always make my bed and put my things away. I sometimes take out the trash. I feed and walk our dog. I never do the dishes because we have a dishwasher. But I take the dishes out of the dishwasher and my mother puts them away.

How I helped people last week

Last week, I helped my grandmother to use the computer. And I helped my mother to carry grocery bags from the supermarket. At school, I cleaned the bookshelves in our English classroom, and I picked up litter from the playground.

My ideas for helping people in our community

IDEA 1

We all have toys that we don't want. I think we can put all our unwanted toys in boxes and give them to a children's hospital.

IDEA 2

We all have books we don't need any more. We can organize a book sale at school. We can give the money we raise to charity.

by Becky

30 **Plan your project.**

THINKING SKILLS
Analyzing

1. How do you help at home?
2. How did you help people last week?
3. How can your class help the community?
4. Write and present your project.

You can also present your project in this way.

AB page 62

Do the Unit 6 Review and Self-assessment (Activity Book page 62). Complete your *Progress Journal* for Unit 6.

7 A camping trip

AIMS

In this unit:

- I **name** and **describe** camping equipment.
- I **listen to** and **read** a photo story *The tiger thieves.*
- I **talk about** plans in the future.
- I **find out about** places to visit in the US.
- I **talk about** going to middle school in a role play.
- I **read about** dramatic weather, and **write** and **present** a project.

Lesson 1

1 04:05 **Listen and say.**

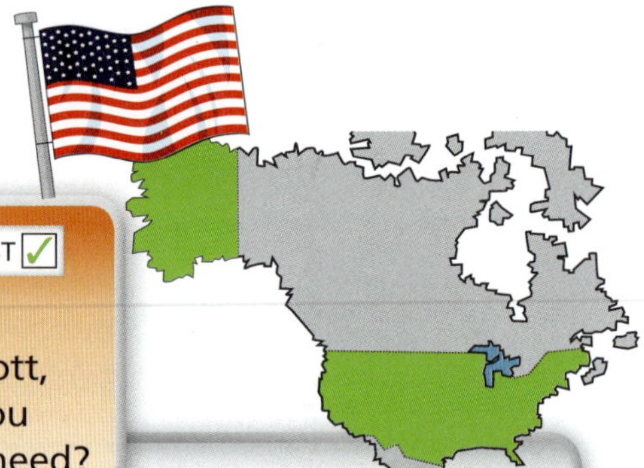

Tiger Tracks SLN POST

Hi, everyone – Becky here. I'm going to go camping in Yellowstone National Park, out west in the US, with Scott, Florence, Finn, Ed and Zoe. Which of these things do you think I need to take? Can you think of anything else I need?

1 
waterproof jacket

2 
blanket

3 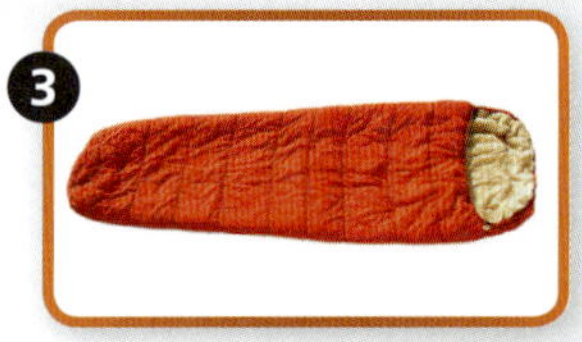
sleeping bag

4 
tent

5 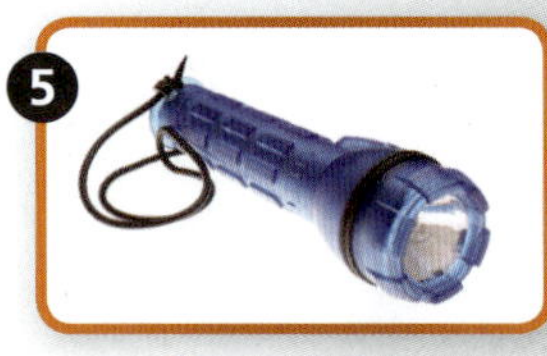
flashlight

6 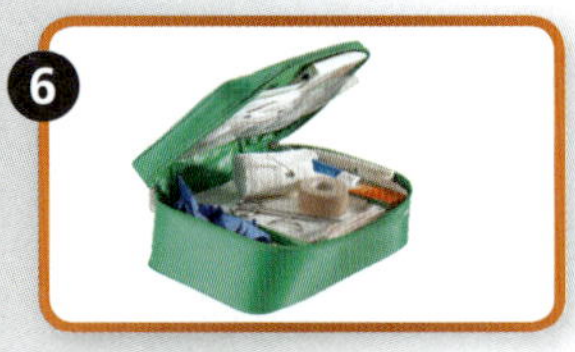
first aid kit

7 
towel

8 
toothbrush and toothpaste

9 
pocketknife

10 
map and compass

2 **Discuss with a partner. Write your ideas.** 04:06 **Now listen and find out.**

I think she needs to take a flashlight.

I agree. A flashlight is important. I don't think she needs to take a pocketknife.

3 04:07 **Listen and do the vocabulary quiz.** ?

This is big and flat. You put it on your bed when it's cold.

INTERNET TRACKS Look at a map of the US. Find Yellowstone National Park. How far is it from New York to Yellowstone?

Lesson 2

POST ✓

We're at the campsite. It's at Bridge Bay, near a big lake. The wilderness is really beautiful! This is the list of the campsite rules. Do you think they are good rules?

4 Listen and read. 04:08

READING TIP Use the pictures to help you guess the meaning of new words.

A

B

C

Welcome to the Bridge Bay Campsite.

Please read the list of rules.

Campsite rules

1. Please keep the campsite clean. Do not drop litter. Use the trashcans and recycling bins.
2. Please do not make noise, especially at night when people are asleep.
3. Do not play ball in the tent area. You can play ball in the open fields.
4. Do not make fires to cook. There is a barbecue area in the campsite where you can prepare food.
5. When you leave the campsite, always tell someone where you are going.
6. Please respect the forest and the wilderness around the campsite.

Please follow these rules. They help us make the campsite a safe and happy place.

We hope you are going to have a fantastic vacation.

Mr Thompson

Director of the Bay Bridge Campsite

D

E

F

THINKING SKILLS
Remembering and memorizing

5 Look at the pictures. Say the rules.

6 Play *Dictate and write.* Beat the clock.

Do not play ball in the tent area.

7 Think and say.

TALK ABOUT IT!

'Please keep the campsite clean.' This is a good rule because nobody wants to see litter on the campsite.

INTERNET TRACKS Find out how Yellowstone got its name.

Lesson 3

8 Listen to and read the story. 04:10

POST ✓

Hi everyone. I'm writing this from the campsite. This photo story is about an adventure we had yesterday. I hope you enjoy it.

The tiger thieves

- What do the tiger thieves have?
- Do the children catch the thieves?

The children are having breakfast at the campsite. They are talking about what they are going to do.

1

2

3

4

9 **Read and answer the questions.**

1 How many tiger cubs are missing from the wildlife park?
2 What time is the van going to come to the campsite?
3 What do the children think is in the van?
4 Why do the man and woman want the toy tigers?
5 Are the man and woman angry with the children?
6 What are the children going to do with their toy tigers?

Tiger Values
Think about it!

Is it important to protect endangered species? Why?
What can you do to protect wildlife where you live?

5

6

7

8

9

Do you know...?

In the year 1900, there were approximately 100,000 tigers in the world. Today, there are less than 4,000.

TALK ABOUT IT!

10 Ask and say.

1 Do you like the story? Why? / Why not?
2 What's your favorite part of the story?
3 Do you think the children were right to tell Mr Thompson about the man and the woman?
4 Do you want to go on a camping trip in the US?

Everyday phrases: learn and use!

That's an excellent idea!
Oh no! That's terrible.
I don't believe it!
It doesn't matter.

Lesson 4

11 04:11 **Listen and read. Is Becky worried about middle school? Does Ed like his school?**

Ed: What **are** you **going to do** after this vacation?
Becky: In September, **I'm going to start** middle school.
Ed: Are you worried about it?
Becky: No. I think it**'s going to be** great. My best friend **is going to be** with me. We**'re going to have** new teachers and we**'re going to make** new friends. We**'re going to study** interesting new subjects. And we think the school uniform is really cool.
Ed: That's good.
Becky: What about you? **Are** you **going to start** middle school this year?
Ed: No. I started last year.
Becky: Really? Do you like it?
Ed: I love it. All the teachers are great. And I love learning German and French.

12 **Act out the dialogue. Change the words to make it true for you.**

13 04:12 **Listen, repeat and learn.**

going to

I'm	going to	study new subjects.
He's / She's		make new friends.
You're / We're / They're		have new teachers.

I'm not	going to	study new subjects.
He / She isn't		make new friends.
You / We / They aren't		have new teachers.

Are you	going to	start middle school?	Yes,	I am.	No,	I'm not.
Is he / she		wear a new uniform?		he / she is.		he / she isn't.

14 **Be a grammar detective! Look at page 67 in the AB.**

Do we use *going to* + verb to talk about the past or the future?

What verb do we always use before *going to*?

How many examples of *going to* + verb can you find in the story?

FAST TRACK GRAMMAR *Write five sentences about what you're going to do after school today.*

Lesson 5

Sound track /ə/

15 04:14 **Listen and identify. Listen and repeat.**

What are you going to do today?

I'm going to read a book.

I'm going to take photos.

I'm going to walk the dog.

I'm going to play chess.

I'm going to watch a movie.

I'm not going to do anything.

16 04:15 **Listen and say *True* or *False*. Correct the false sentences.**

	Saturday		Sunday	
Jack			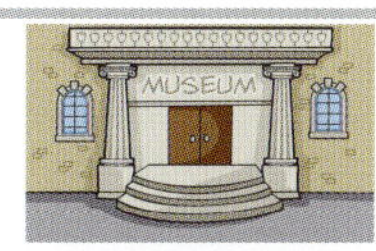	
Jane			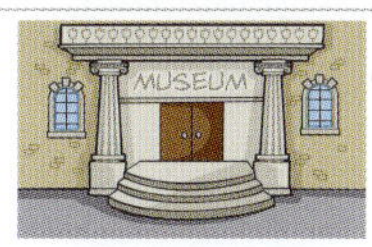	
Zach				
Annie				

17 **Play *Who am I?***

Are you going to play tennis on Saturday?

Yes, I am.

Are you going to go to a concert on Sunday?

No, I'm not.

You're Jane!

Yes, that's right!

18 **Talk about you and your friends.**

I'm going to play soccer tonight.
Toby is going to watch the soccer game.

TALK ABOUT IT!

FAST TRACK GRAMMAR *Write five sentences about your friends' plans for this weekend.*

Hello, everyone! Here's an excellent website that we're using to plan our vacation. Guess what we're going to do tomorrow.

POST ✓

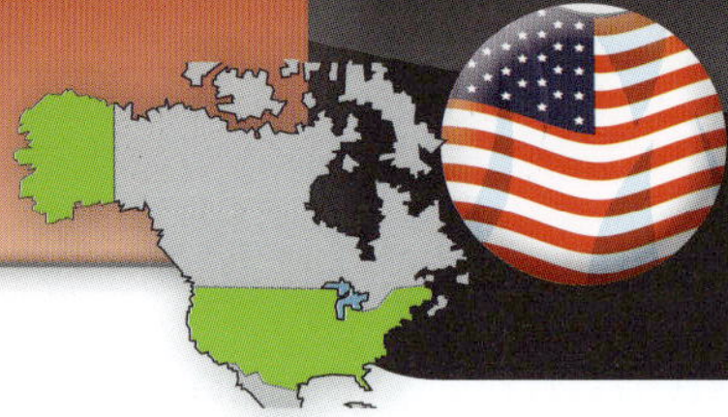

Lesson 6

19 04:17 **Listen and read.**

Things to do in Yellowstone

1 Play some sports in Yellowstone National Park
The National Park is an outdoor paradise for sporty people. There are paths where you can go hiking, biking and horseback riding. You can also go rock climbing and canoeing. But the best thing about the park is the beauty of the wilderness. It's spectacular!

2 Travel by train
If you don't like hiking, a journey by train is a great way to see the wilderness. You can see the beautiful mountains and valleys from the comfort of your train.

3 Go shopping in Yellowstone
Yellowstone has a lot of gift shops. It's the perfect place to buy your souvenirs. And when you need a break, you can stop for a sandwich and a drink.

4 Visit Old Faithful Geyser
Old Faithful is Yellowstone's most famous geyser. The geyser erupts every half hour to two hours. The eruptions can go as high as 56 meters for as long as five minutes. Old Faithful's water can be as hot as 118 °C far underground.

5 Spend time watching wildlife
Yellowstone has 60 species of mammals, including bison, elk, moose, wolves, bears, deer, sheep, and mountain lions. Herds of bison move freely in the park and there are 30,000 elk. There are also 600 grizzly bears. Watch out!

6 Hike the Petrified Forest
Yellowstone's Specimen Ridge has the largest number of petrified trees in the world. There are more than 100 fossilized plant species. The forest was created 50 million years ago from volcanic eruptions.

7 Visit Yellowstone's Grand Canyon
Yellowstone's Grand Canyon is 39 kilometers long, 370 meters deep, and 1.2 kilometers wide. The canyon was created by glaciers.

20 **What are they going to do?** 04:18 **Listen and answer.**

Scott and Zoe	are going to	go biking in the wilderness	tomorrow.
Ed and Finn		go shopping in Yellowstone	
Becky and Florence		visit Old Faithful Geyser	
		travel by train	
		visit Yellowstone's Grand Canyon	

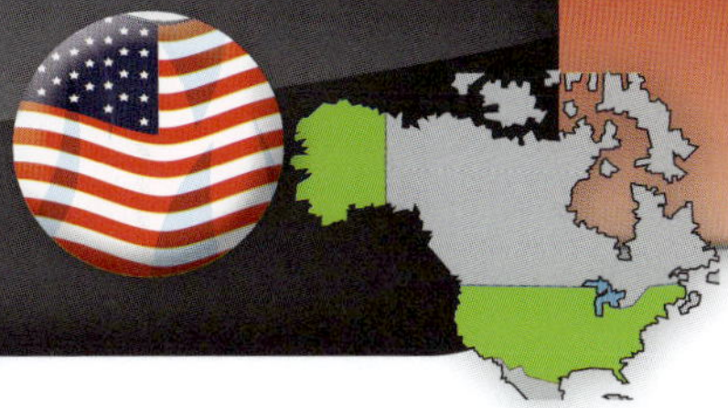

POST ✓

Here's a group photo of us in a café in Yellowstone on the last day of our camping trip. Read and find out our opinions of the vacation.

Lesson 7

21 04:19 **Listen and read.**

What were their favorite places in Yellowstone?
Which activities did they enjoy doing?

One day, we traveled by train. I think old trains are fantastic, so that was my favorite activity. And the most interesting place was the petrified forest. I really like nature. I think some of the trees were amazing. Really cool.

The best activity for me was rock climbing. I had a really good instructor and we climbed for three hours. The most interesting place for me was the lake. There were so many amazing animals to look at. It's a beautiful place.

I liked all the places we visited. But number one for me was the shopping in Yellowstone. I love shopping! And my favorite activity was cooking at the campsite. I helped prepare some of the meals. It was fun.

I really enjoyed biking in the wilderness. Yellowstone is very green. The views are spectacular. My favorite activity? I think it was watching wildlife. We saw some awesome animals, especially the big bison. They all looked really healthy and happy.

I really enjoyed hiking in the wilderness because Yellowstone is so beautiful. The views are incredible. But my favorite place was Old Faithful Geyser. I love history, so it was really interesting. It was amazing to see something so old.

We also went to Yellowstone's Grand Canyon. I think that was my favorite activity. I didn't know Yellowstone had a canyon. And I think my favorite place was the campsite. I loved it. It was a lot of fun. The drama with the tiger cub toys was exciting, too. And now we all have fantastic souvenirs!

22 04:20 **Listen and say *True* or *False*. Correct the false sentences.**

TALK ABOUT IT!

23 **Say where you want to go and what you want to do in Yellowstone.**

I want to go shopping in Yellowstone and see Old Faithful.

CLIL

Geography

Lesson 8

24 Listen and read. 04:21

The weather forecast was very important during our vacation in Yellowstone, so I'm posting this article about weather stations and weather forecasts. Do you know who writes the weather forecast? Read and find out. POST

What do meteorologists do?

Meteorologists study the weather. They receive information from weather stations about changes in temperature, air pressure, wind and rain. They also study images of the Earth from satellites. The meteorologists use this information to understand how our climate works, and to write weather forecasts.

What are weather forecasts?

Weather forecasts tell us what the weather is going to be like. Many people listen to weather forecasts on the radio or on television. You can also find weather forecasts online or in newspapers.

The weather forecast can help everyone make simple decisions such as what to wear, or where to go on the weekend. But for some people, the weather forecast is very, very important. Pilots and sailors need to know about storms and strong winds before they can travel. Farmers need to know about rain, heatwaves and hailstorms to protect their animals and crops. Forest rangers and firefighters need to know about heatwaves to prevent and put out forest fires.

Thunder and lightning

Lightning is electricity that comes from a storm cloud. It's extremely hot. It's hotter than the surface of the sun! Thunder is the sound of air moving very quickly. It happens when lightning strikes.

Heatwaves

A heatwave is when the temperatures are higher than normal for a long period of time.

Hailstorms

In a hailstorm, small balls of ice fall from the sky. Sometimes, the balls of ice can be bigger than golf balls!

Tornados

A tornado is a column of spinning air. The top touches storm clouds and the bottom touches the ground. Tornados can move at more than 300km an hour.

25 **Read and answer.**

1 What do meteorologists study?
2 What else do meteorologists do?
3 Where can you read a weather forecast?
4 Who needs to know about…
- heatwaves
- thunder storms
- tornados
- hailstorms

26 **Play *Association*.**

THINKING SKILLS Associating

Lightning.

It's extremely hot.

It's electricity.

It's frightening.

27 **Think and say.** My world

What's the weather like today?

Are there sometimes tornados, storms and heatwaves where you live?

My words to remember

hailstorm thunder lightning weather forecast tornado heatwave

INTERNET TRACKS Find out the size of the biggest hailstone in history.

Project: Planning a weekend away

28 04:22 **Listen and read.**

I'm going to go away for the weekend with my mom. This is what we're going to do. Do you like our plans? POST ✓

What I'm going to do

Next weekend, I'm going to go to New York City with my mother. We're going to take the train from Washington, DC on Friday after school. It leaves at five fifteen. It arrives in New York at eight thirty. The journey takes nearly four hours, so we're going to take books to read on the train. And we're going to take sandwiches and drinks.

In New York City, we're going to stay with my aunt, my mother's sister. We're going to visit the Empire State Building on Saturday morning. After that, we're going to go shopping in Times Square. I want to buy some earrings. In the evening, we're going to see a play on Broadway.

On Sunday we're going to walk in Central Park before lunch. Then, in the afternoon, we're going to catch the train back to Washington, DC.

The weather forecast says that it's going to be cloudy but it isn't going to rain. I think we're going to have a fantastic weekend!

By Becky

29 **Plan your project.**

THINKING SKILLS
Planning

1. **Decide where to go and how to get there.**
2. **Decide what you're going to do at your destination.**
3. **Check the weather forecast.**
4. **Write and present your plans.**

You can also present your project in this way.

➔ AB page 72

Do the Unit 7 Review and Self-assessment (Activity Book page 72). Complete your *Progress Journal* for Unit 7.

World Music Day

1 Listen and read. 04:25

POST ✓

Hi, everyone! World Music Day is a celebration of music all over the world. This website tells you about how we celebrate World Music Day in the US! I hope you like it.

What is World Music Day?

World Music Day is a festival on June 21st every year. It started in France over thirty years ago. Some people wanted to have a special day when everyone could listen to music. All the events in the festival were free. The musicians didn't have to pay for a place to perform. They could play anywhere – inside a building or outside on the street!

Today, this festival is popular in many countries around the world. Many musicians want to play their music on this day. But there are two important rules. The first rule is that the festival has to be on June 21st – the beginning of summer in the US. The second rule is that all events must be free so anyone can take part, and anyone can watch.

Many bands and musicians play music all night! And there is music for everyone – from classical music to rap and jazz.

Do you celebrate World Music Day in your country? Where do you like to listen to music?

2 Listen and read. 04:26

POST ✓

Hello again! This year, for World Music Day, we are going to listen to the lyrics of a special song!

Listen to the music
Floating through the air,
I can hear melodies
From everywhere, from everywhere.

Look at the musicians
Dressed in black and white,
Listen to them play
All through the night.

Listen to the music
Floating through the air,
I can hear clapping
From everywhere, from everywhere,

Look at all the children
Dancing to the beat,
Listen to the sound
Of all the stomping feet!

Listen to the music
Floating through the air,
I can feel the rhythms
From everywhere, from everywhere.

Inventor's Day

1 Listen and read. 04:27

Hi there! In the UK and US, people celebrate Inventor's Day on February 11th every year. This is one of my favorite days because at school we make our own inventions! Here's an excellent website where you can find out all about it.

POST

The origins of Inventor's Day

Inventor's Day is on February 11th. This is the date when Thomas Edison was born in 1847. He was a brilliant American scientist and he invented many different objects. Today we still use many of these objects. His most famous invention was an electric light bulb.

New inventions, like the light bulb, made people's lives easier and better. Some of the first inventions were thousands of years ago, for example, the wheel.

The wheel was a very important invention because it helped people travel from one place to another, to carry heavy loads and to make pottery. Today, cars, buses, trains, planes and bikes all use the wheel. Can you imagine life without these things?

People invented many other machines and objects a long time ago, like paper, pottery, glass and cloth. We still use these inventions today. Can you think of other examples?

Inventions today

Some inventions can also cause problems. For example, many machines use raw materials like coal, gas and wood. These resources are running out and they can also cause pollution. Many inventors today are trying to invent objects and machines that use resources that do not pollute the air, like solar power.

How do you celebrate Inventor's Day in your country? What important inventors or inventions do you know?

2 Listen and read. 04:28
Make a special invention.

Hi! We made an invention at school today. We used beans, some plastic wrap and a plastic cup. Can you guess what our invention is? This is how to make it!

POST

How to make a percussion instrument

You need:
- a clean, empty yogurt cup or plastic food container
- some plastic wrap
- a marker
- a large rubber band
- scissors
- some dry rice or beans

What to do
1. Cut off a piece of plastic wrap.
2. Put the cup or container face-down on the plastic wrap.
3. Draw around the shape of the cup or container, 8 cm from the edge.
4. Cut out the shape you drew on the plastic wrap.
5. Put the rice or beans into the container.
6. Stretch the plastic wrap tightly over the end of the container and hold it in place with the rubber band.
7. Shake your percussion instrument to make a sound!

Independence Day

1 Listen and read. 04:29

Hi there! In Mexico, September 16th is a very important day. It's Independence Day! Here's a blog to tell you all about it! POST ✓

Mexican Independence Day

Over two hundred years ago, Mexico was a Spanish colony. The Spanish government ruled the country, but the people living in Mexico didn't like the Spanish government. Life was hard for many Mexicans. They thought there were too many laws and these laws took away their freedom.

In 1810, many people in Mexico decided they wanted to be an independent country.

They fought for a long time against the Spanish. Eleven years later, in 1821, Mexico was free from Spain and became an independent nation.

Today, Mexicans all over the world celebrate Mexican Independence Day on September 16th. The celebrations begin before midnight on September 15th, when the president says 'El Grito' in the main square in Mexico City, the capital. During this speech he talks about the heroes of the independence, and finishes by saying 'Viva Mexico!' three times. A lot of people watch this on television and, the next day, there are parades all over the country. People wear traditional costumes and decorate their homes and cars with Mexican flags. Thousands of people come to Mexico City. During the parades, bands play music and people wave flags. Everyone has a good time. After, many families celebrate with food and songs. There are also concerts and fireworks.

Do you have a national day or a special day that you celebrate every year in your country? When is it?

2 Listen and read. Make a golden eagle. 04:30

Hello! Did you know that the national bird of Mexico is the golden eagle? This beautiful bird is North America's largest bird of prey. Would you like to make your own golden eagle? Here is how to make it. POST ✓

How to make a golden eagle

You need:

- the eagle template
- scissors
- paints, crayons or colored pens
- glue

What to do

1. Cut out the eagle template.
2. **Color** or paint your eagle. Color the head light brown and the beak yellow and white.
3. **Color** or paint the top part of the wings dark brown and the bottom part light brown and white.
4. **Color** the body dark brown.
5. Color the claws orange and the tail black and white.
6. Roll the eagle's body into a cylinder and stick the ends together.
7. Stick on the head, wings, claws and tail.

Fabulous!

Songs bank

Everyone's welcome at our youth club

04:31

I like running, climbing. I love scuba diving.
My sister likes painting, writing and designing.
My brother likes playing the clarinet.
I have a friend. He likes using the internet.

Chorus
Musical, technical, scientific,
Adventurous, sporty or artistic.
We're all different, that's OK.
We don't want to be the same.
Everyone's welcome at our youth club.
Our super cool, very cool after school youth club.
Everyone's welcome at our youth club.

I like juggling, swimming. I love going fishing.
My sister likes reading, singing and just thinking.
My brother likes playing basketball,
And I have a friend. She doesn't like sports at all.

Chorus

My *superhero*

04:33

Some superheroes can climb mountains high.
Some superheroes can fly in the sky.
Some can jump as high as they please.
Some can save the forests and the trees.

My best friend cannot climb.
He isn't strong. He cannot fly.
But my best friend is very kind.
He's the kindest, most generous person I know.
My best friend is my superhero!
My super, super superhero!

Some superheroes can catch waterfalls.
Some superheroes can crash into walls.
Some can lift a thousand kilos.
Some can stop erupting volcanoes.

My best friend cannot climb.
She isn't strong. She cannot fly.
But my best friend is very kind.
She's the kindest, most generous person I know.
My best friend is my superhero!
My super, super superhero!

04:35 Chocolate cake

Let's bake,
Let's bake.
Let's make a cake.
A cake for friends and family.
A cake we can have with a cup of tea.
A cup of tea.

There's some flour,
There are eggs,
There's some sugar and spice.
There's some butter and ***chocolate***,
Mmmm! That's very nice.

Put it in a bowl,
Mix it with a spoon,
Put it in the oven,
And very, very soon, you have a ***chocolate*** cake.
A ***chocolate*** cake.
Yeah! Everybody loves a ***chocolate*** cake.
Mmmm! Delicious.

*(Repeat, replacing **chocolate** with **coffee**)*

04:37 WHO HAS THE STATUE?

THE DAILY NEWS

STATUE MISSING

At three ten yesterday afternoon the statue of the president was in the center of the square. At three twenty, the statue was missing. Where were you at three fifteen yesterday afternoon? Did you see the robbery? Do you know who has the statue?

Chorus
Who has the statue?
Who? Who? Who?
Did you take the statue?
Was it you, you or you?

It wasn't me.
I wasn't there.
I was nowhere near the square.
I was at the theme park at three fifteen.
You can ask my sister.
She was there with me.

Chorus

It wasn't me.
I wasn't there.
I was nowhere near the square.
I was at the airport at three fifteen.
You can ask my brother.
He was there with me.

Chorus

Inventions, inventions

04:39

Chorus
Inventions, inventions, some are truly great.
The microwave, the dictionary and the rollerskate.
Inventions, inventions, some are truly hip.
The microscope, the microphone and the paperclip.

What did Graham Bell invent?
Was it something great?
Where did he invent it?
And do you know the date?

Chorus

What did Roland Hill invent?
Was it something great?
Where did he invent it?
And do you know the date?

Chorus

What did Orville Wright invent?
Was it something great?
Where did he invent it?
And do you know the date?

Chorus

We're gonna go camping

04:41

Chorus
We're gonna go camping in the country.
We're gonna sleep in a tent tonight.
We're gonna go camping in the country.
We're gonna have fun on a campsite.

I'm packing a pocketknife. I'm packing a rope,
Toothbrush and toothpaste and some soap.
I think I have everything I'm gonna need.
Don't forget to take a book to read.

Chorus

I'm packing a blanket. I'm packing my shoes,
Sunglasses, sunscreen and shampoo.
I think I have everything. I have it all.
Don't forget to take a bat and ball.

Chorus

I'm packing a compass. I'm packing a map,
Waterproof jacket and a cap.
I think I have everything. I think that's it.
Don't forget to take a first aid kit.

Chorus

gonna = going to

Vocabulary

Unit 1

1 Look and match.

a

b

c

d

e

1 go to pop concerts
2 do puzzles
3 collect things
4 play the drums
5 juggle
6 use the internet
7 make things
8 play chess
9 go fishing
10 practice a foreign language

f

g

h

i

j

2 Read and write the correct verb.

~~juggle~~ go do collect play use make play go practice

1 I ___juggle___.
2 I ________ chess.
3 I ________ the drums.
4 I ________ puzzles.
5 I ________ stickers.
6 I ________ the internet.
7 I ________ models.
8 I ________ to pop concerts.
9 I ________ a foreign language.
10 I ________ fishing.

Unit 2

1 Look and write.

1 
yevall
valley

2 
setder
____

3 
taerfwlla
____

4 
nraitorsfe
____

5 
lffic
____

6 
calvono
____

7 
andisl
____

8 
evac
____

9 
lacrieg
____

10 
tmnouani ganre
____
____

2 Match the sentences to the words.

1 A place between two hills.
2 A place surrounded by the ocean.
3 This is made out of ice.
4 It doesn't rain very often here.
5 This is where a river falls off a mountain.
6 A lot of tropical plants grow here.
7 The Alps are an example of this.
8 This can be inside a mountain.
9 These are often by the ocean.
10 This can be active or dormant.

a island
b rainforest
c cave
d cliffs
e volcano
f desert
g glacier
h mountain range
i waterfall
j valley

Vocabulary

Unit 3

1 Look and write.

~~coconuts~~ coffee honey citrus fruits olives sugar rice beans spices salt

1 
coconuts

2 
______

3 
______

4 
______

5 
______

6 
______

7 
______

8 
______

9 
______

10 
______

______

2 Look at the food and drink in Activity 1. Write.

Foods I eat	Foods I don't eat	Foods that grow in my country

Unit 4

1 Look and match.

a 

b 

c 

d 

e 

1 airport
2 botanical garden
3 sports stadium
4 post office
5 tourist information office
6 bank
7 theme park
8 shopping center
9 main square
10 port

f 

g 

h 

i 

j 

2 Match the sentences to the words.

1 A place with a lot of plants and trees.
2 A place where people go to mail letters.
3 A place where people go to get information about a place.
4 A place with a lot of attractions and rides.
5 A place where people keep their money.
6 A place where people go to watch soccer or baseball.
7 A place with a lot of boats and ships.
8 A place with a lot of stores.
9 A place in the center of a town where people can meet.
10 A place where planes land and take off from.

a airport
b botanical garden
c sports stadium
d post office
e port
f bank
g theme park
h shopping center
i main square
j tourist information office

Vocabulary

Unit 5

1 Look and match.

a

b

c

d

e
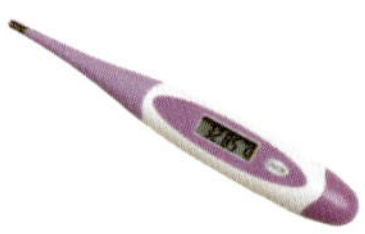

1 light bulb
2 stamps
3 umbrella
4 dishwasher
5 Band-Aids
6 paper clip
7 microwave
8 microscope
9 bilingual dictionary
10 digital thermometer

f

g
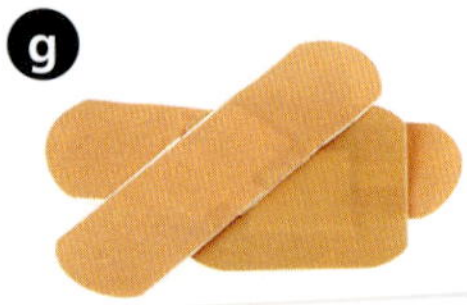

h

i

j
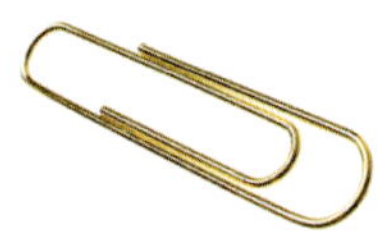

2 Read and write *True* or *False*.

1 Stamps are to send letters. True
2 A light bulb is to cook food. ______________
3 A paper clip is to hold paper together. ______________
4 An umbrella is for when it's raining. ______________
5 A dishwasher is for washing clothes. ______________
6 A microwave is to cook food. ______________
7 A microscope is for looking at very small things. ______________
8 A bilingual dictionary is to find the translation of words. ______________
9 Band-Aids are to mend furniture. ______________
10 A digital thermometer is to check body temperature. ______________

Vocabulary

Unit 6

1 **Look and write. Match.**

~~do~~ take clean feed wash sweep put clean make water

a

b

c
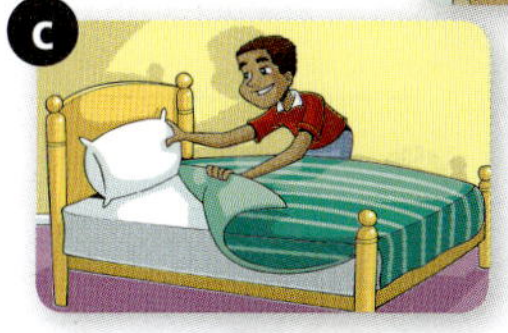
d

e

1 ___do___ the dishes
2 __________ your bed
3 __________ out the trash
4 __________ the plants
5 __________ up
6 __________ the windows
7 __________ the car
8 __________ the floor
9 __________ the pets
10 __________ your clothes away

f

g

h

i

j

2 **Look at the chores in Activity 1. Write.**

Things I do at home	Things I don't do at home

Vocabulary

Unit 7

1 Look and write.

first aid kit towel ~~blanket~~ map and compass tent flashlight
toothbrush and toothpaste waterproof jacket pocketknife sleeping bag

1 

blanket

2 

3 

4 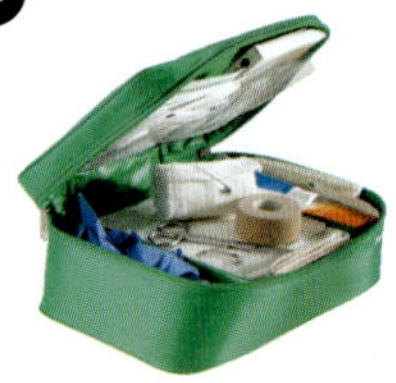

5 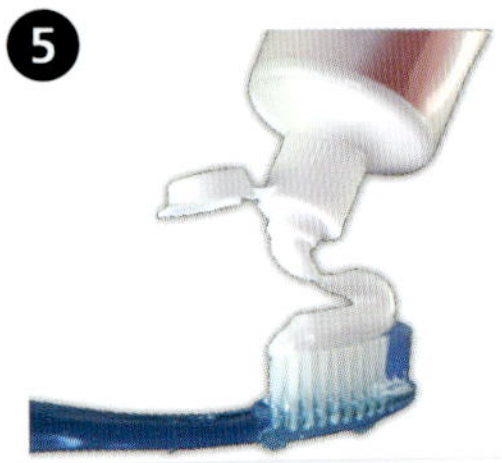

6 

7 

8 

9 

10 

2 Match the sentences to the words.

1 You need this if it's cold. (1 — j)
2 You need this to see in the dark.
3 You need these to find the right direction.
4 You need this if someone has an accident.
5 You need this to cut food.
6 You need this to wear if it rains.
7 You need this to sleep in.
8 You need this to live in when you go camping.
9 You need this after a shower.
10 You need these to keep your teeth clean.

a flashlight
b sleeping bag
c map and compass
d pocketknife
e tent
f toothbrush and toothpaste
g first aid kit
h towel
i waterproof jacket
j blanket

Verb List

- to add ______
- to attract ______
- to blow ______
- to celebrate ______
- to chat ______
- to clean the windows ______
- to collect things ______
- to conjugate verbs ______
- to cook ______
- to decorate ______
- to deliver ______
- to demonstrate ______
- to develop ______
- to do puzzles ______
- to do the dishes ______
- to erupt ______
- to escape ______
- to feed the pets ______
- to give presents ______
- to give thanks (for the harvest) ______
- to give up (your free time) ______
- to go fishing ______
- to go online ______
- to go to pop concerts ______
- to grow ______
- to harm ______
- to have a competition ______
- to have dinner ______
- to help ______
- to improve ______
- to juggle ______
- to knock (on the door) ______
- to look up (opening times) ______
- to make things ______
- to make your bed ______
- to meet ______
- to pick up litter ______
- to play a musical instrument ______
- to play chess ______
- to play games ______
- to play (practical jokes) ______
- to play the drums ______
- to practice a foreign language ______
- to prefer ______
- to prevent (forest fires) ______
- to protect (animals and crops) ______
- to put your clothes away ______
- to receive information ______
- to recycle (paper) ______
- to save (a life) ______
- to save time ______
- to send (an email) ______
- to solidify ______
- to stick ______
- to study ______
- to sweep the floor ______
- to take out the trash ______
- to talk ______
- to clean up ______
- to train a dog ______
- to travel ______
- to treat (a patient) ______
- to use the internet ______
- to walk the dog ______
- to wash the car ______
- to watch TV ______
- to water the plants ______
- to write a blog ______

These verbs are irregular. Write the past forms.

- to blow ______
- to do ______
- to feed ______
- to give ______
- to go ______
- to grow ______
- to have ______
- to make ______
- to meet ______
- to put ______
- to read ______
- to send ______
- to speak ______
- to stick ______
- to sweep ______
- to take ______
- to write ______

Grammar Reference

Unit 1 *like + ...ing*

Grammar presentation

Remember! When a short verb ends with a consonant, a vowel and a consonant, we double the final consonant.

Affirmative and negative sentences

I You We They	like don't like	swimming. collecting stamps. playing the drums. talking to friends going to concerts. making things.
He She	likes doesn't like	

Questions

What do	you they	like	doing?
What does	he she		

Do	you they	like	making things? swimming? going to concerts?
Does	he she		

Grammar check

1 **Write *like* or *likes*.**

1 Do you ___like___ doing puzzles?
2 I don't ________ swimming.
3 My sister ________ making cakes, but she doesn't ________ eating them!
4 What do you ________ doing?
5 What does your brother ________ doing on the weekend?
6 He ________ going to concerts.
7 Helen doesn't ________ collecting stamps.
8 What do they ________ doing after school?
9 Does Igor ________ playing the drums?
10 We ________ going fishing.

2 Write the *ing* forms.

double the consonant and add ing	take away the e and add ing	just add ing
swim → swimming	make → making	learn → learning
store → ______	have → ______	collect → ______
chat → ______	juggle → ______	play → ______
run → ______	practice → ______	go → ______
put → ______	explore → ______	listen → ______

3 Write the *ing* forms. Use the table in Activity 2 to help you.

1 I like juggling.

2 I don't like ______.

3 I like ______ stamps.

4 I like ______ chess.

5 I don't like ______.

6 I like ______ things.

4 Match the questions and answers.

1 What do you like doing after school?
2 Do you like going to concerts?
3 Does your sister like speaking English?
4 What does your mom like doing?
5 Do your friends like listening to music?
6 Does your dad like playing chess?

a Yes, she does.
b She likes playing the piano.
c I like watching TV.
d No, he doesn't.
e Yes, they do.
f No, I don't.

5 Answer the questions about yourself.

1 What do you like doing after school? I like ______
2 Do you like using the internet? ______
3 Do you like cooking? ______
4 What do you like doing on the weekend? ______

Grammar Reference

Unit 2 Superlative adjectives

Grammar presentation

Short superlative adjectives (with *est*)

- Mount Cook is the highest mountain in New Zealand.
- The largest volcano in New Zealand is called Mount Ruapehu.
- The howler monkey is the noisiest animal in the world.
- The kakapo is the heaviest species of parrot.

Long superlative adjectives (with *most*)

- The Waitomo Caves are one of the most popular tourist attractions in New Zealand.
- The most venomous animal in the world is the box jellyfish.
- The Moa was a big bird. It lived in New Zealand. The most interesting fact about the Moa is that it didn't have any wings.

Grammar check

1 Match the adjectives to their opposites.

1 short 2 interesting 3 easy 4 cheap

a difficult b long c expensive d boring

2 Write the superlative adjectives.

Short adjectives	
long	the longest
short	______
easy	______
cheap	______

Long adjectives	
boring	the most boring
difficult	______
interesting	______
expensive	______

3 Look at the information about the books. Then read and circle.

Long or short?	91 pages	237 pages	380 pages	158 pages
Interesting or boring?	7/10	5/10	9/10	10/10
Difficult or easy?	★★★★	★★★	★	★★
Cheap or expensive?	$6	$9	$8	$4

★★★★ = very difficult ★ = very easy

1 The blue book is **the most interesting** / **the most boring** book.
2 The yellow book is **the longest** / **the shortest** book.
3 The purple book is **the easiest** / **the most difficult** book.
4 The red book is **the cheapest** / **the most expensive** book.

4 Complete the sentences.

1 The yellow __________ book is the easiest book.
2 The __________ book is the most expensive book.
3 The __________ book is the shortest book.
4 The __________ book is the most interesting book.

5 Complete the sentences to make them true. Use superlative adjectives.

tall ~~long~~ high deep

1 The Nile is the longest __________ river in the world.
2 Mount Everest is __________ mountain in the world.
3 The Pacific Ocean is __________ ocean in the world.
4 The giraffe is __________ animal in the world.

6 What do you think? Write.

1 I think the __________ is the most interesting animal in the world.
2 I think the most popular building in my town is the __________.

Grammar Reference

Unit 3 Countable and uncountable nouns

Grammar presentation

	Uncountable nouns
Affirmative	There is some flour.
Negative	There isn't any honey.
Questions	Is there any butter?

	Countable nouns	
	Singular nouns	Plural nouns
Affirmative	There is a packet of flour.	There are some strawberries.
Negative	There isn't an orange.	There aren't any oranges.
Questions	Is there a bottle of milk?	Are there any eggs?

We can't count flour, but we can count packets of flour!
We can't count milk, but we can count bottles of milk!

Grammar check

1 **Circle the things you can count.**

milk (apple) pasta butter orange packet of pasta juice banana

flour grape olive oil packet of sugar bottle of olive oil sugar egg

2 **Complete the sentences. Write *a, an, any* or *some*.**

	Uncountable nouns	Countable nouns	
		Singular nouns	Plural nouns
Affirmative	There is _some_ juice.	There is ______ bottle of milk.	There are ______ oranges.
Negative	There isn't ______ milk.	There isn't ______ packet of flour.	There aren't ______ eggs.
Questions	Is there ______ flour?	Is there ______ apple?	Are there ______ grapes?

3 Find and circle five differences.

4 Write *A* or *B*.

1 There is some honey. Picture __A__

2 There is one bottle of milk. Picture ____

3 There is some sugar in a bowl. Picture ____

4 There are five bananas. Picture ____

5 There are some grapes. Picture ____

6 There is a pineapple. Picture ____

5 Look at Picture B. Write *a* or *any*. Then circle *yes* or *no*.

1 Are there __any__ bananas? yes / no

2 Is there ________ bowl? yes / no

3 Is there ________ sugar? yes / no

4 Is there ________ honey? yes / no

5 Is there ________ pineapple? yes / no

6 Are there ________ grapes? yes / no

6 Look at the picture. Circle the correct words.

1 There is / are an / some eggs.

2 There is / are a / some banana.

3 There is / are an / some milk.

4 There is / are a / some flour.

5 There is / are an / some cherries.

6 There is / are an / some apples.

Grammar Reference

Unit 4 The past simple (*was, were*)

Grammar presentation

Questions

Where	were	you they	at 5:35 yesterday?
	was	he she	

Were	you they	at the library? at school? at home?
Was	he she	

Affirmative and negative sentences

I He She It	was wasn't	at the movie theater at a friend's house at the park at the airport at school	at	7:20 6:00 14:10 12:55	yesterday.
We You They	were weren't				

Three oh five = five minutes **after** three o'clock.
Two fifty five = five minutes **before** three o'clock.

Grammar check

1 Order and write questions.

1 at / were / on Wednesday afternoon? / you / three fifty / Where
Where were you at three fifty on Wednesday afternoon?

2 the / Were / airport? / you / at ______

3 Anna / seven o'clock / Where / yesterday evening? / at / was /
______

4 she / shopping center? / at / Was / the / ______

5 Monday morning? / were / Where / at / they / nine twenty / on
______

6 school? / they / at / Were ______

7 yesterday? / was / at / five ten / he / Where
______

8 park? / Was / he / in / the ______

2 Look. Circle *was* or *were*. Write the places.

sports stadium   swimming pool   ~~post office~~   museum   library   movie theater

1 Where **was** / **were** Lily at three oh five? She **was** / **were** at the <u>post office</u>.

2 Where **was** / **were** Ben and Lily at seven thirty? They **was** / **were** at the ____________________.

3 Where **was** / **were** Ben at ten o'clock? He **was** / **were** at the ____________________.

4 Where **was** / **were** Lily and Ben at one fifty five? They **was** / **were** at the ____________________.

3 Write *was, were, wasn't* or *weren't*.

1 Ben and Lily <u>weren't</u> at the supermarket at seven thirty.

2 Lily __________ at the museum at ten o'clock.

3 Ben __________ at the sports stadium at five o'clock.

4 Lily and Ben __________ at the park at eleven twenty.

4 Complete the answers.

1 Was Ben at the post office at three oh five? <u>No</u>, he <u>wasn't</u>.

2 Were Ben and Lily at the swimming pool at one fifty five? __________, they __________.

3 Was Lily in the supermarket at twelve thirty five? __________, she __________.

4 Were Lily and Ben at the movie theater at ten o'clock? __________, they __________.

5 Was Lily in the museum at eleven twenty? __________, she __________.

Grammar Reference

Unit 5 Past simple questions

Grammar presentation

When a question starts with ***Did***, the answer is usually ***Yes*** or ***No***.

Questions and answers

–	Did	Jenner he	live in England? discover a vaccination theory? live in the 20th Century?	Yes, he did. No, he didn't.

***Wh*-questions in the past**

Where What When	did	Jenner he	live?
			work?
			discover?
			do in 1784?
			die?

Grammar check

1 Match the questions and answers.

1 Where did George Lerner live? — c
2 What toy did he invent?
3 When did he invent it?
4 What happened in 1952?

a Mr Potato Head.
b In 1949.
c In the US.
d Mr Potato Head appeared on television.

5 Where did Leonardo da Vinci live?
6 What was his most famous painting?
7 When did he paint it?
8 When did he die?

e Between 1503 and 1506.
f In Italy.
g In 1519.
h The Mona Lisa.

2 Complete the questions. Write *What*, *When* or *Where*.

1 Where ____________ did Thomas Edison live? In the US.

2 ____________ did he do in 1871? He married his first wife.

3 ____________ did he marry his second wife? In 1885.

4 ____________ did he invent? A lot of useful things.

5 ____________ did he invent his light bulb? In New Jersey.

6 ____________ did he die? In 1931.

3 Order, write and match.

1 George Lerner / invent? / What / did
What did George Lerner invent?

2 did / die? / When / Edward Jenner
____

3 the phonograph? / invent / Did / Edison
____

4 Where / live? / did / Josephine Cochrane
____

5 Leonardo da Vinci / design? / did / What
____

a In 1823.

b A flying machine.

c Yes, he did.

d A type of toy.

e In the US.

4 Write true answers.

1 What did you do this morning before school?
____

2 Did you do your homework yesterday?
____

3 Where did you go for your last vacation?
____

4 What did you do last weekend?
____

5 Did you go to the beach last summer?
____

Grammar Reference

Unit 6 The past simple (irregular verbs)

Grammar presentation

Every day

Do	you	make your bed?	Yes, I do. / No, I don't.
	I	make my bed. take out the trash. feed the dog.	
	I don't	make my bed. take out the trash. feed the dog.	

Yesterday

Did	you	make your bed?	Yes, I did. / No, I didn't.
	I	made my bed. took out the trash. fed the dog.	
	I didn't	make my bed. take out the trash. feed the dog.	

Grammar check

1 **Write the irregular past forms. Look at the table on page 89 to check your answers.**

Infinitive	Past
ride	rode
take	________
go	________
swim	________
eat	________

Infinitive	Past
draw	________
write	________
have	________
drink	________
make	________

2 **Complete the text with the correct infinitive or past form. Remember to use the infinitive after *didn't*.**

On Wednesday, Evan (*go*) (1) went ____________ to the beach with his friend Mark. They (*ride*) (2) ____________ their bikes. They didn't (*swim*) (3) ____________ in the ocean, but they (*make*) (4) ____________ a big sandcastle. Then they (*have*) (5) ____________ lunch. Evan (*eat*) (6) ____________ a sandwich, but he didn't (*eat*) (7) ____________ any chips. He (*drink*) (8) ____________ some juice. He didn't (*take*) (9) ____________ any photos, but he (*draw*) (10) ____________ a picture of the beach.

3 **Read the text in Activity 2 and complete the answers.**

1 Did Evan and Mark go to the park on Wednesday? No ________, they didn't ____________.
2 Did they swim in the ocean? ____________, they ____________.
3 Did they make a sandcastle? ____________, they ____________.
4 Did they have lunch at the beach? ____________, they ____________.
5 Did Evan take any photos? ____________, he ____________.
6 Did he draw a picture? ____________, he ____________.

4 **Write four true sentences about yesterday. Choose past forms and infinitives from above.**

1 I ____.
2 I ____.
3 I didn't ____.
4 I didn't ____.

Grammar Reference

Unit 7 *going to*

Grammar presentation

Affirmative sentences

I'm You're He's / She's We're / They're	going to	start middle school in September. have new teachers. study new subjects. make new friends.

If you know the verb **be**, it's easy to use **going to**!

Negative sentences

I'm not You aren't He / She isn't We / They aren't	going to	study new subjects. make new friends. learn a foreign language. be at elementary school in September.

Questions and short answers

Am I Are you	going to	start middle school in September? have new teachers? learn a foreign language? be at elementary school in September?	Yes, I am. / No, I'm not.
Is he / she			Yes, he / she is. / No, he / she isn't.
Are we / they			Yes, we / they are. / No, we / they aren't.

Grammar check

1 Change these affirmative sentences to negative sentences.

1 He's going to play basketball.
He isn't going to play basketball.

2 I'm going to learn a foreign language.
____

3 We're going to go camping.
____

4 It's going to be sunny tomorrow.
____

2 What are they going to do? Look, read and complete the sentences.

play table tennis ~~ride a bike~~ go ice skating
take a photo write an email make a sandwich

1 George is wearing a helmet. *He's going to ride a bike.* ______

2 Martha has a camera. *She's going to* ______

3 Pam and Jack have ice skates. *They're* ______

4 John is looking at his laptop. *He* ______

5 Linda has some bread. *She* ______

6 Sam and Kate have bats. *They* ______

3 Look at Activity 2. Complete the answers.

1 Is Linda going to make a sandwich? *Yes*, she *is*.

2 Are George and Martha going to write an email? ______, they ______.

3 Is George going to ride a bike? ______, he ______.

4 Are Pam and Jack going to go ice skating? ______, they ______.

5 Is John going to take a photo? ______, he ______.

6 Is Kate going to play table tennis? ______, she ______.

4 Answer the questions.

1 Are you going to go shopping today? ______

2 Are you going to be at elementary school next year? ______

3 Is it going to rain tomorrow? ______

4 Is your teacher going to be at school tomorrow? ______

5 Are you going to go camping this summer? ______

6 Are you going to write any emails this evening? ______

Reading 1

1 Read.

The biggest, the fastest and the youngest!

A lot of people collect things such as stamps, stickers or bottles. Some people collect strange things. Val Kolpakov, in the US, collects toothpaste tubes. He has the biggest collection of toothpaste tubes in the world! He has more than 2,000 and they're from all over the world – from countries such as Japan, Korea, China, India and Russia.

Many children love skateboarding. Do you have a skateboard? How big is it? The biggest skateboard in the world is in the US. A group of people made it in 2009, and it was on TV. The skateboard is 11.14 meters long and 1.1 meters high! And what about the fastest skateboarder? Mischo Erban, who lives in Canada, skateboarded at 129.9 kilometers per hour in 2012. That's fast!

Do you like drums? The biggest drum in the world is in South Korea. It's 5.5 meters wide and six meters tall. The youngest professional drummer in the world is Julian Pavone, who was born in 2004 and lives in the US. He started playing when he was only three months old!

2 **Which of these records are mentioned in the text? Check.**

1 the youngest professional drummer ✓
2 the biggest skateboard ☐
3 the fastest skateboarder ☐
4 the biggest stamp collection ☐
5 the youngest professional skateboarder ☐
6 the biggest drum ☐
7 the fastest drummer ☐
8 the biggest collection of toothpaste tubes ☐

3 **Complete the sentences using phrases from Activity 2.**

1 The biggest skateboard in the world is in the US.
2 The ______________________ in the world lives in Canada.
3 The ______________________ in the world is in the US.
4 The ______________________ in the world was born in 2004.
5 The ______________________ in the world is in South Korea.

4 **Write the numbers.**

1 How old was Julian Pavone when he started to play the drums? three months
2 How wide is the biggest drum in the world? __________ meters
3 How many toothpaste tubes does Val Kolpakov have? More than __________
4 How fast did Mischo Erban skate in 2012? __________ kilometers per hour
5 How long is the biggest skateboard in the world? __________ meters

5 **Match.**

1 The biggest skateboard in the world	come from all over the world.
2 The biggest drum in the world is	stamps.
3 A lot of people collect	was born in 2004.
4 Mischo Erban is the	was on TV.
5 Val Kolpakov's toothpaste tubes	fastest skateboarder in the world.
6 The youngest professional drummer in the world	six meters tall.

Reading 2

1 **Read.**

Visit Kenya ... the most exciting country in Africa!

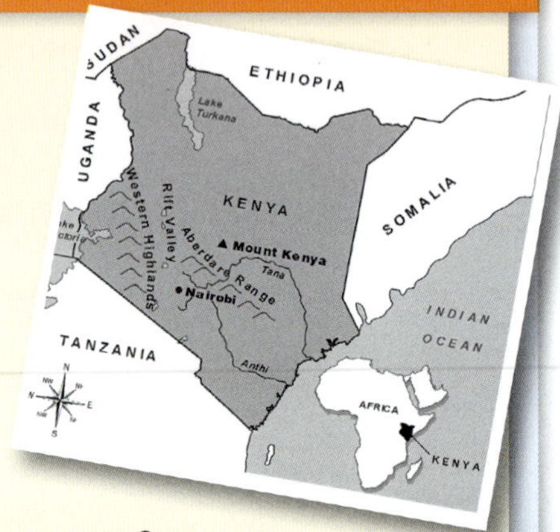

See Mount Kilimanjaro

Mount Kilimanjaro is in Tanzania but you can see it when you're in Kenya. It's a volcano and it's the highest mountain in Africa. The weather in Kenya is always hot but there's always snow on Mount Kilimanjaro!

Stay in Nairobi

Nairobi, the biggest city in Kenya, has hundreds of stores and cafés. Explore the city and stay in one of its wonderful hotels.

Go to the beach

Kenya has more than 500 kilometers of beautiful beaches. The sand is white and the ocean is blue! You can go swimming, snorkeling or surfing.

Go on safari

Kenya has many national parks, where you can see fantastic animals. See the 'big five': buffalo, lions, elephants, leopards and rhinos. Stay at a campsite or in a hotel.

Visit Lake Turkana, the biggest lake in Kenya

Go fishing by boat, or visit Central Island and see the dangerous crocodiles!

2 Find the words in the text. Write.

1 

hotel

2 

____

3 

____

4 

____

5 

____

6 

____

7 

____

8 

____

9 

____

10 

____

11 

____

12 

____

3 Read the text and complete the sentences. Write one adjective on each line.

fantastic ~~beautiful~~ dangerous wonderful hot

1 Kenya's beaches are beautiful.
2 The crocodiles in Lake Turkana are ______________.
3 The hotels in Nairobi are ______________.
4 The weather in Kenya is ______________.
5 The animals in the National Parks are ______________.

4 Answer the questions.

1 What's the name of the highest mountain in Africa? Mount Kilimanjaro
2 What's the name of the biggest city in Kenya? ______________
3 What's the name of the biggest lake in Kenya? ______________
4 What's the name of the island where you can see crocodiles? ______________
5 What can you always see on Mount Kilimanjaro? ______________
6 What do you think is the most interesting thing to do in Kenya? ______________

____

Reading 3

1 **Read.**

What's your favorite dessert?

We asked three American adults this question. Here are their answers:

A

Martin, San Diego

My favorite dessert is apple pie. I'm really good at making it! There's pastry on the top and bottom of the pie. I make the pastry with flour, butter and sugar. In the middle, I put apples, spices and sugar. I often make apple pie for my family on Sundays. I eat it with ice cream because I don't like whipped cream. It's delicious!

B

Elsa, Miami

My favorite dessert is a banana split. When I was a child, I always had this dessert on my birthday. It's fun to make. First, cut a banana, and put some ice cream in the middle. Then put some whipped cream on top. I add cherries, nuts and chocolate syrup too. Try it – it's the best dessert in the world!

C

Kevin, Boston

My favorite dessert is Black Forest cake. People first started to make this cake in Germany. To make it, you need flour, sugar, butter, eggs, cherries, chocolate and cream. It isn't difficult to make. I love cherries and chocolate, so this dessert is perfect for me!

2 Find the ingredients in the text. Which desserts have the ingredients? Write A, B or C.

A = apple pie   B = banana split   C = Black Forest cake

1
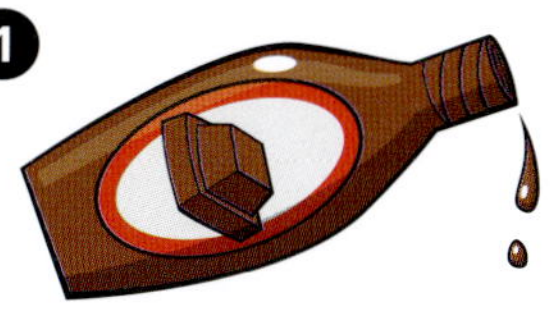
chocolate syrup
Dessert B

2

whipped cream
Desserts ____, B and C

3

____
Dessert ____

4

____
Desserts ____ and ____

5
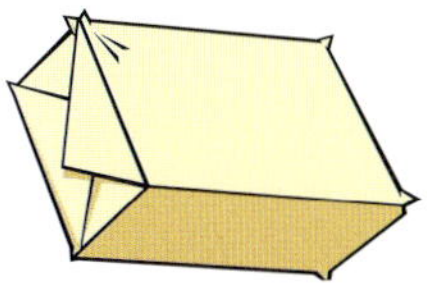
____
Desserts ____ and ____

6

____
Desserts ____ and ____

7

____
Desserts ____ and ____

8

____
Dessert ____

9

____
Dessert ____

10

____
Dessert ____

11

____
Dessert ____

12

____
Dessert ____

3 Answer the questions. You don't need to write sentences.

1 What's Elsa's favorite dessert? banana split
2 Who can make pastry? ____________
3 Who's from Boston? ____________
4 Where's Martin from? ____________
5 Who doesn't like whipped cream? ____________
6 What kind of syrup does Elsa put on her dessert? ____________
7 Which desserts have cherries in them? ____________
8 Why is Black Forest cake perfect for Kevin? ____________

4 What is your favorite dessert? Write.

My favorite dessert is ____________.

To make it, you need ____________

____________.

Reading 4

1 **Read.**

Dear Katie,

In July I went to a language school in New York. I was there for two weeks. I stayed with a host family, who lives in an apartment in the city. They have two sons called Jacob and Max. Jacob is twelve - the same age as me.

I had English lessons every morning. We had three teachers. The lessons were fun because we played a lot of games. The teachers said, "Speak English, please!". I learned a lot of new words.

In the afternoons and on the weekend we visited a lot of places. One afternoon we had a picnic at a beautiful beach in the Hamptons. On another afternoon, we went to the Chrysler Building. It is over 85 years old!

Jacob's family has a sailboat. One weekend we sailed to Liberty Island. This island is very small and it is home to the famous Statue of Liberty.

On the last day, I went to Long Island Wildlife Park with Jacob's family. It's not very big. You can see hundreds of animals including an 18-foot giraffe, red kangaroos, kinkajous, cougars, Barbados sheep, peacocks, and the only lemurs born and bred on Long Island.

I really enjoyed my time in New York.. I want to go again next year!
Karl

2 Complete the crossword with words from the text.

Down ↓

1 

3 

6 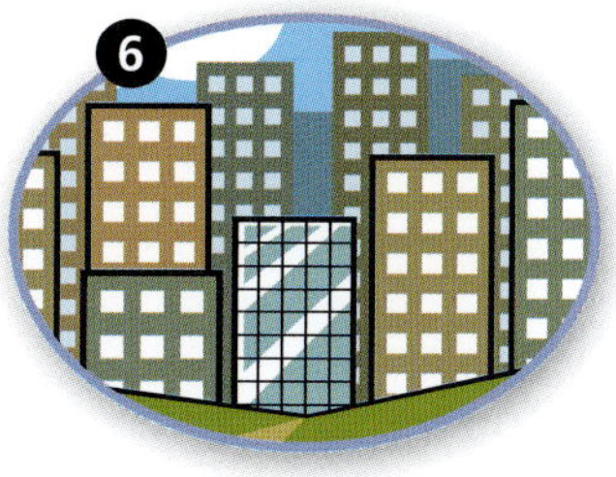

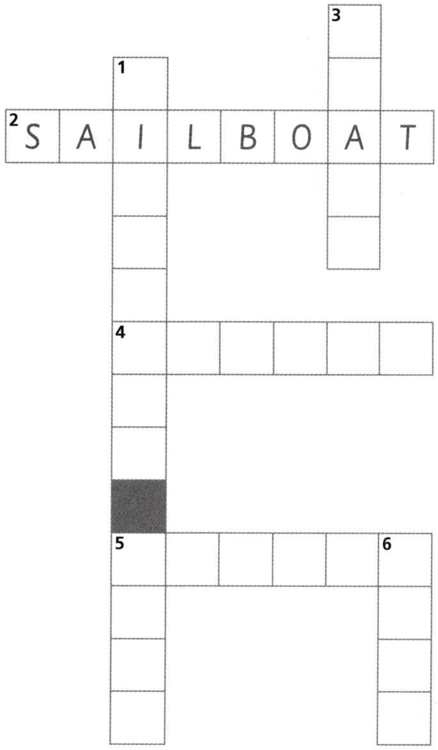

Across →

2 

4 

5 

3 Read the text and circle the correct words.

1 Jacob and his family live in a **house** / **apartment**.
2 Jacob has one **brother** / **sister**.
3 Karl and Jacob had a picnic at a **beach** / **park**.
4 Karl went to Staten Island by **car** / **boat**.
5 They went to the wildlife park on the **first** / **last** day.
6 They went to **the Chrysler Building** / **Central Park**.
7 Karl wants to go to **New York** / **Scotland** next year.

4 Answer the questions. You don't need to write sentences.

1 What's the name of the city where Jacob's family lives? New York
2 How many children are there in the host family? ______________________
3 Did Karl enjoy his English lessons? ______________________
4 What kind of boat does Jacob's family have? ______________________
5 Where can you see a lot of birds? ______________________
6 How old is the Chrysler Building? ______________________

Reading 5

1 **Read.**

A wonderful vacation

We interviewed Katie, age 12, about her summer vacation last year.

Hi, Katie. Can you tell me what you did last summer?

OK. I went camping with my parents and my brother in Wales. We go there every year. It often rains there. I don't like the rain but the countryside is beautiful.

Do you go to the same campsite every year?

Yes, we do. It's in a forest and it's really nice. There's water there, but there isn't any electricity.

Oh! How do you cook?

We cook on a fire. It's fun.

Who does the dishes?

I do. I don't like doing the dishes at home, but I like doing it when I'm camping.

What do you do in the evenings?

Well, we don't listen to music or use our cell phones, because we can't use the chargers! But I have a flashlight, so I can read a book, and sometimes we play games.

Where is the campsite?

It's near Snowdon, which is the highest mountain in Wales. Last year we went to the top of the mountain. We were lucky – it didn't rain that day! The view was amazing! We could see Ireland!

There's a train that goes to the top of the mountain. Did you go on the train?

No, we didn't. We walked up. A lot of people go on the train, but I love walking.

What do you like best about camping?

Sleeping in a tent.

2 Write the words. Find and color the words in the green box below. Use the other letters to complete Katie's sentence.

1 

e*lectricity*

2 

f______________

3 

f______________

4 

w______________

5 

b______________

6 

c______________

Don't use the letter x.

B	T	D	O	I	X	F	W	A	T	E	R
O	C	A	M	P	S	I	T	E	S	N	Y
O	E	L	E	C	T	R	I	C	I	T	Y
K	U	X	F	O	R	E	S	T	R	C	E

Katie loves the ______________ near Snowdon!

Tip: The word is in the text. It has 11 letters.

3 Complete the paragraph.

walked forest mountain ~~camping~~ train cooked

Katie and her family went (1) *camping* in Wales last summer. The campsite is in a (2) ______________. They (3) ______________ on a fire. One day they went up Snowdon, which is a big (4) ______________. Katie (5) ______________ up the mountain, but a lot of tourists go on the (6) ______________.

4 Does Katie like these things? Put a check in the correct box.

	Yes	No	Don't know
the campsite	✓		
sleeping in her bed			✓
sleeping in a tent			
rain			
snow			

	Yes	No	Don't know
doing the dishes at home			
doing the dishes at the campsite			
swimming			
walking			
cooking on a fire			

Reading 6

1 **Read.**

My fantastic invention

This is Norbert, my robot. He's incredible!

Norbert can walk and he can talk. He can do a lot of things, and he is very helpful. Every morning, when I get up, he makes my bed. Then he cleans up my bedroom and puts my clothes away. We go downstairs and he makes breakfast for my family. He's very good at cooking eggs and making toast. We don't need a dishwasher, because Norbert does the dishes! He feeds the dog and the cat, and he takes out the trash. He washes and irons our clothes, and he sweeps the floor.

Norbert has a lot of interesting gadgets in his body. Inside his head there's an amazing computer. Norbert goes to school with me and helps me with my work, and he does my homework for me. His favorite subject is math. It isn't difficult for him! He speaks all the languages in the world, and he can write too. There's a thermometer in one of his legs. When it's cold, he gives me a sweater. When it's hot, he opens the window. In his other hand, there's a cell phone. He can send text messages and phone my friends. After school I often watch TV. But I don't watch the TV in the living room. Norbert has a TV in his tummy!

by Anthony

2 What can Norbert do? Write the verbs.

He can …

1 ___speak___ a lot of languages.
2 ________ Anthony's bedroom.
3 ________ eggs.
4 ________ Anthony's clothes away.
5 ________ Anthony's friends.
6 ________ the floor.
7 ________ Anthony's homework.
8 ________ breakfast.
9 ________ Anthony's bed.
10 ________ all the clothes.
11 ________ toast.
12 ________ the dog and the cat.
13 ________ text messages.
14 ________ out the trash.

3 What gadgets does Norbert have in his body? Check.

1 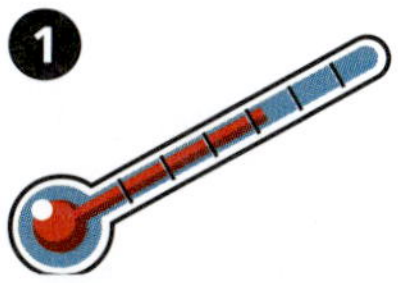
thermometer ☑

2 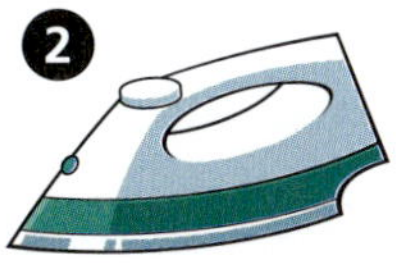
iron ☐

3 
dishwasher ☐

4 
cell phone ☐

5 
computer ☐

6 
toaster ☐

7 
TV ☐

4 Answer the questions. You don't need to write sentences.

1 What three things does Norbert do in Anthony's bedroom?
makes Anthony's bed, ________

____

2 Who sweeps the floor in Anthony's house? ________
3 What's in Norbert's head? ________
4 What's Norbert's favorite subject? ________
5 Can he speak English? ________
6 What does Norbert do when it's cold? ________

Speaking 1

Talking about things you're good at

1 Complete the dialogue. Use the words in the box. Prepare to speak

juggle	~~sporty~~	favorite	drums	badminton	subjects

A: What sports are you good at?

B: I'm not very (1) ___sporty___. But I'm okay at (2) ______________.

A: Are you musical?

B: Yes, I am. I play the (3) ______________ and I'm good at singing too.

A: What school (4) ______________ are you good at?

B: I'm good at math and music. And I'm really good at art, too. Art is my (5) ______________ subject.

A: What else can you do?

B: I can (6) ______________ with three balls!

2 Match to complete the dialogue.

1 Are you creative? — d
2 Are you technical?
3 Are you good at doing puzzles?
4 Are you good at English?
5 Can you play chess?

a No, I'm not. I don't understand machines and computers.
b Yes, I can. But I'm not very good at it.
c No, I'm not. I hate them!
d Yes, I am. I'm really good at art and I like making things.
e Yes, I am. It's my favorite subject.

3 What are you good at? Make lists.

I'm very good at these things: ______________________________

____

I'm quite good at these things: ______________________________

____

4 Talk with your partner about things you're good at. Use the questions in Activities 1 and 2 to help you.

Speaking 2

Talking about a country

1 **Number the continents on the map.** Prepare to speak

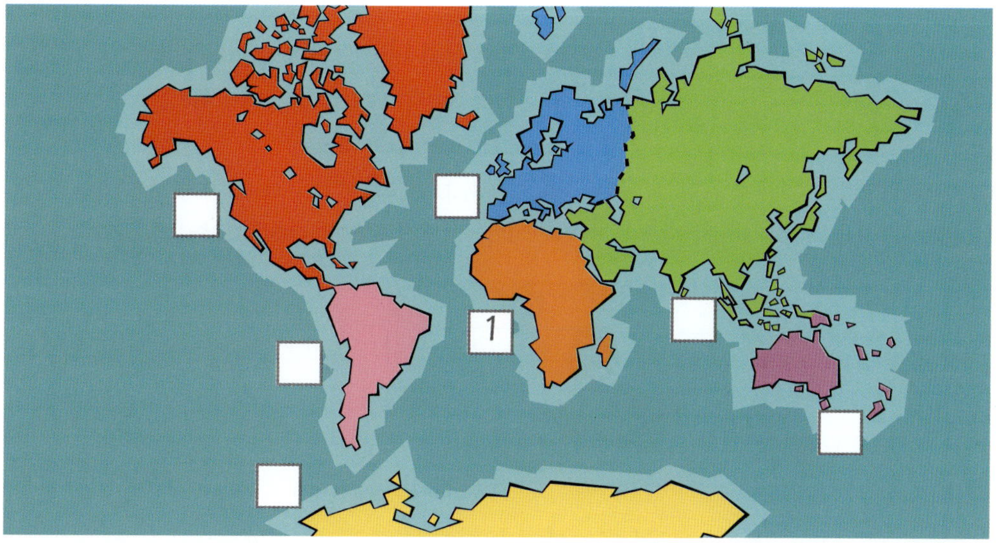

1 Africa
2 Antarctica
3 Asia
4 Australia
5 Europe
6 North America
7 South America

2 **Choose a country and find out about it. Draw the flag. Write notes.**

Country: ______________________

Continent: ______________________

Population: ______________________

Languages: ______________________

Other interesting information: ______________________

____

3 **Match the questions and answers.**

1 What country did you find out about?
2 What continent is it in?
3 What colors are on the flag?
4 What's the population?
5 What languages do people speak there?
6 What else do you know about it?

a Blue, yellow and red.
b French and Arabic.
c Chad.
d There is an enormous lake called Lake Chad.
e Africa.
f 11 million.

4 **Ask and answer questions about the country you found out about. Use the questions in Activity 3.**

Speaking 3

Ordering food in a café

1 Match the questions and answers. Prepare to speak

1 Good morning. What you would you like?
2 With peas?
3 Would you like a drink?
4 Would you like a dessert?
5 Which kind of cake would you like?

a Yes, I'd like some cake, please.
b No, with spinach, please.
c Lemon, please.
d Yes, please. I'd like some water.
e I'd like chicken and rice, please.

2 Complete the dialogue. Use the words in the box.

please like ~~fries~~ No juice thanks would

A: Good afternoon. What would you like?
B: Sausages and (1) _fries_, please.
A: Would you like salad with that?
B: No, (2) ________. I'd like carrots, please.
A: Would you (3) ________ a drink?
B: Can I have an apple (4) ________, please?
A: And (5) ________ you like a dessert?
B: Yes, I'd like a vanilla ice cream, (6) ________.
A: Would you like anything else?
B: (7) ________, thanks.

3 Act out the dialogue with your partner. Choose food from the menu. Use the dialogues above to help you.

Speaking 4

Sequencing events in the past

1 **Complete the dialogue. Use the words in the box.** Prepare to speak

amazing	home	~~went~~	play	concert	watched	Where	shoes

A: Where did you go on Saturday?

B: In the morning I (1) ___went___ to the sports center to (2) ________ tennis.

A: Where did you go in the afternoon?

B: First I went to the shopping center to buy some
(3) ________.

A: (4) ________ did you go after that?

B: I went to the square in the town to watch a pop
(5) ________.
It was (6) ________! Then I went home.

A: Where did you go in the evening?

B: I stayed at (7) ________ after dinner. I was tired!
I (8) ________ a DVD.

2 **Find and complete the time phrases from the dialogue.**

1 on Saturday

2 in the m________

3 in the a________

4 f________

5 after t________

6 t________

7 in the e________

8 after d________

3 **Read and match.**

1	I went to the post office	to have a picnic.
2	We went to the supermarket	to look at the dinosaurs.
3	I went to the bus station	to buy some stamps.
4	I went to the museum	to watch a soccer game.
5	We went to the sports stadium	to catch a bus.
6	We went to the botanical garden	to buy some vegetables.

4 **Act out a dialogue. Use the questions in Activity 1 and time phrases in Activity 2 to help you.**

Speaking 5

Talking about a famous person from history

1 **Find out about a famous person from the past. Write notes.** Prepare to speak

Name: ______________________________

Lived (where): ______________________________

Famous because: ______________________________

Born (when): ______________ Died (when): ______________

Other interesting information: ______________________________

____

2 **Match the questions and answers.**

1 What famous person did you find out about? — d
2 Why was he famous?
3 Where did he live?
4 When was he born?
5 When did he die?
6 What else do you know about him?

a Because he painted amazing abstract pictures.
b In 1973. He was 92.
c In France and Spain.
d Pablo Picasso.
e His father was an art teacher.
f In 1881.

3 **Look at the pictures and write the names.**

a 
b 
c 
d 
e 

Hernán Cortés	Mother Teresa	Anna Pavlova	Marilyn Monroe	Neil Armstrong

1 *Mother Teresa* was famous because she helped poor people in India.

2 ______________ was famous because he was the first person to stand on the moon.

3 ______________ was famous because she acted in a lot of movies.

4 ______________ was famous because he explored Mexico.

5 ______________ was famous because she was an amazing dancer.

4 **Ask and answer questions about the famous person you found out about. Use the questions in Activity 2.**

Speaking 6

Looking for things and borrowing things

1 Read the questions. Cross out the answer that isn't possible. Then check your answers with your partner. Prepare to speak

1 Can you see my pocketknife?
- a Yes, I can. It's under your bed.
- ~~b Yes, you do.~~
- c No, sorry.

2 What are you looking for?
- a In the first aid kit.
- b My toothbrush.
- c The map.

3 Where's the compass?
- a It's in my backpack.
- b I don't know.
- c No, I'm not.

4 Can you pass me the map, please?
- a No, thanks.
- b Sorry, I'm looking at it.
- c Yes, here you are.

5 Can I use your flashlight, please?
- a OK.
- b No, there isn't.
- c Yes, of course.

2 Complete the questions and answers. Use the words in the box.

please ~~know~~ pass it's for go Sorry Can

Where's my sleeping bag? I don't (1) ___know___. Is it in the tent?

What are you looking (2) ______? My backpack.

Can you (3) ______ me the pocketknife, please? (4) ______, I'm using it.

(5) ______ you see my towel? Yes, (6) ______ on your bed.

Can I use your blanket, (7) ______? OK! Here you (8) ______.

3 Ask and answer questions about these classroom objects.

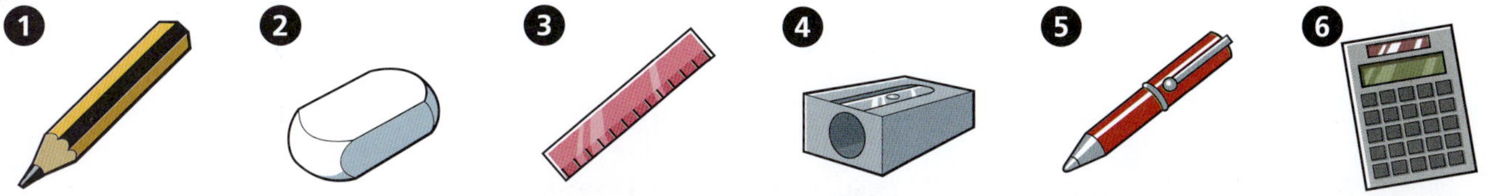

1 pencil 2 eraser 3 ruler 4 sharpener 5 pen 6 calculator

Study Skills 1

Using a dictionary: checking spelling

1 **Put these words in alphabetical order. Then find them in your dictionary. Write a translation.**

sporty artistic creative scientific musical ~~adventurous~~ technical

	Word	Translation
1st	adventurous	
2nd		
3rd		
4th		
5th		
6th		
7th		

2 **Find and correct the spelling mistakes. Use your dictionary.**

1 I ~~usualy~~ usually go fishing on Saturday mornings.

2 English is a foregn language.

3 I want to buy a tickit for the soccer game.

4 We're collecting glass bottels.

5 Who's your favorit singer?

3 **Play a spelling game.**

Practice saying the English alphabet before you start.

Understanding new words in a text

1 **Look quickly at this text.**

What's it about?________________________________

The Shetland pony comes from the Shetland Isles, northeast of mainland Scotland. They are part of the pony family, but their appearance is a bit different. They are short, stocky and have muscular legs - they are very strong! They also have long and thick manes and tails, and a double winter coat to protect them from the harsh weather. Shetland ponies are gentle and intelligent - they are great for children!

When you read a text, try to guess the meanings of words that you don't know. Use the context to help you guess.

2 **Read the text. Don't use your dictionary. Circle five words that you don't know. Use the other information in the sentence to help you guess the meaning.**

My words	Part of speech (noun, verb, adjective, preposition, etc)	What I think it means
stocky	*adjective*	*strong and short*

3 **Check your answers to Activity 2 in your dictionary.**

Remember: When you read a text, don't look up every new word in your dictionary. If you do that, you read very s-l-o-w-l-y!

Study Skills 3

Improving your listening and speaking skills

1 **Draw a picture of one of these things. Include as much detail as possible.**

A person who you know.

A wilderness scene.

A table with food on it.

2 **Describe your picture to your partner. Listen to your partner's description and draw. You can both ask questions.**

3 **Compare pictures. Say what is the same and what is different.**

Here are some more ideas to help you to improve your listening and speaking:

Interview each other for three minutes. Talk about your everyday activities, favorite things, families, etc.

Listen to English or American songs and learn the lyrics. You can find the lyrics on the internet.

Listen to books that have audio CDs, and watch movies and cartoons in English.

Study Skills 4

Using mind maps to record vocabulary

1 **Write each word or phrase in the correct place. Use your dictionary to help you.**

coconuts rice spices ~~chicken~~ bread salt eggs bananas

2 **In your notebook, copy one of these mind maps and add more words, or make your own mind map.**

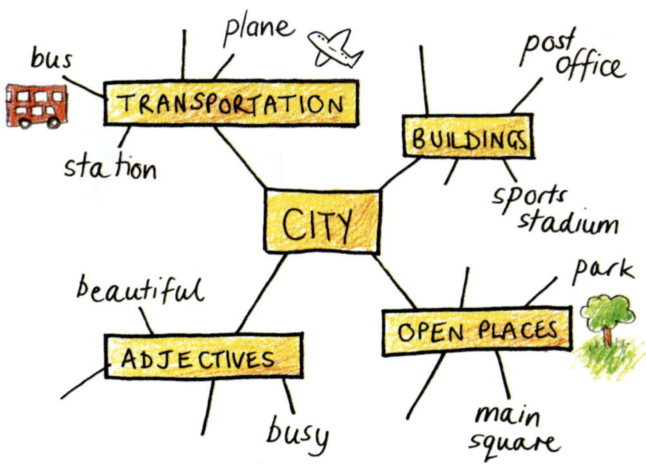

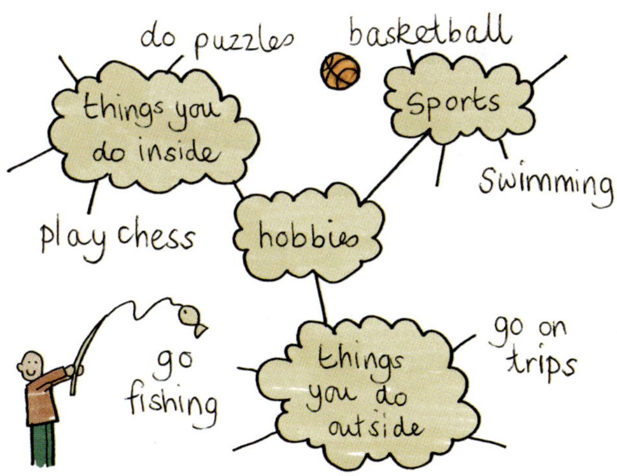

Mind maps are a useful way of recording and organizing vocabulary.

1 Write the name of the topic in the middle.
2 Think about groups of vocabulary in that topic, and write the names in shapes.
3 Add vocabulary to each group. Use your dictionary to add more words.
4 Use a lot of colors and draw pictures. Have fun!

Study Skills 5

Contractions

1 Read and complete the information.

Positive contractions

I + am = I'm

she + is = she's

they + are = they're

Other contractions

was + not = wasn't

can + not = ______

did + not = ______

Negative contractions

I + am + not = ______

she + is + not = ______

they + are + not = they aren't

she + does + not = ______

we + have + do not = we don't have

2 Rewrite the sentences using contractions.

1 He is very creative. He's very creative.

2 My brother does not have a new skateboard. ______

3 Edison did not invent the calculator. ______

4 They are very musical. ______

5 My parents were not at home. ______

3 Look at these sentences. Circle the contraction or possessive 's' and match it to the correct description.

a 's = is

b n't = not

c 's = possessive 's' – not a contraction

1 Katie's happy. [a]

2 He doesn't have math at one twenty. [ ]

3 His skateboard's the fastest. [ ]

4 He doesn't have three older sisters. [ ]

5 Peter's brother is called Paul. [ ]

6 That is Jane's bag. [ ]

Study Skills 6

Improving your writing: using adjectives

1 **Match the adjectives to the correct picture. Add one more adjective to each.**

sunny energetic ~~interesting~~ fruity delicious historical hot friendly

______	*interesting*	______	______
______	______	______	______
______	______	______	______

2 **Look at the text and circle the nouns. Think of adjectives to describe the nouns.**

I went to the (beach) to walk my dog. I sat under a tree and read a book. My dog played with a ball.

nouns	adjectives
beach	*beautiful, sandy*
______	______
______	______
______	______
______	______

3 **Rewrite the text in Activity 2 and make it more interesting. Use the adjectives you found to help you.**

______

______

American Tiger board game

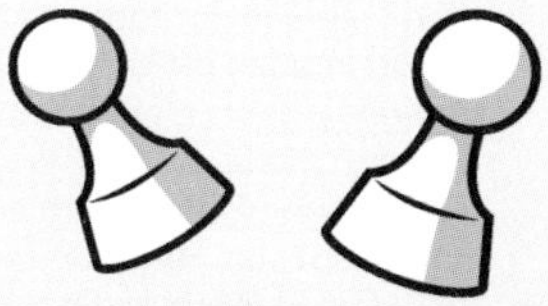

1. Start here! Ask a friend about their interests and ambitions.
2. Say what activities you like doing.
3. Ask a friend what they like doing in their free time.
4. Describe a geographical feature.
5. Go forward one square!
6. Say what foods you like and don't like.
7. Say what places there are in your town.
8. Say where you were at 10:00 and at 18:30 yesterday.
9. Describe an important invention.
10. Go back one square!
11. Ask a friend about the life of an inventor.
12. Say what chores you do at home.
13. Say what you did yesterday.
14. Describe something you need when you go camping.
15. Say what you are going to do on summer vacation.

Macmillan Education
4 Crinan Street
London N1 9XW
A division of Macmillan Publishers Limited

Companies and representatives throughout the world

ISBN 978-1-380-00509-0

Additional material by Kerry Powell
Extra material in the reinforcement section by Kirstie Grainger

This edition published 2017
First edition entitled "Tiger Tracks" published 2014 by Macmillan Publishers Limited
Previous edition entitled "Tiger Time" published 2015 by Macmillan Publishers Limited

Original design by Blooberry Design Ltd
Original page make-up by Andrew Magee Design Ltd
This edition revised and updated by Composure
Illustrated by David Belmonte (Beehive), Humberto Blanco (Sylvie Poggio), Jerome Brasseur (Beehive), Emmanuel Cerisier (Beehive), Kevin Hopgood (Beehive), Martin Impey, Andy Parker, Anthony Rule, Victor Tavares (Beehive)
Original cover design by Astwood Design Consultancy
This edition cover design revised and updated by Andrew Magee Design Ltd
Cover photographs by Corbis, Getty, Stuart Cox, Photodisk, Stockbyte
Picture research by Victoria Gaunt
Original songs and chants arranged and produced by Tom, Dick and Debbie Productions
Recordings produced and arranged by Nerve LLC

Authors' acknowledgments
We would like to thank everyone at Macmillan Education in the UK and in Spain who has helped us in the development and the production of these materials. We would also like to thank all the teachers who have taken time to read, pilot and give feedback at every stage of writing the course. Special thanks from Carol to Alan, Jamie and Hannah for their encouragement and support. Special thanks from Mark to Carlos for his patience and understanding.

The publishers would like to thank the following teachers:
Amparo Fernández Ortiz, CEIP La Patacona, Alboraya, Valencia; Anna Esteban Nieto, Escola Jaume Ferran I Clua, Valldoreix, Barcelona; Carlota López Petidier, CEIP Miguel de Cervantes, Torrejón de Ardoz, Madrid; María del Mar Rodríguez Rodríguez, Escola Els Pins, Barcelona; Mª Inmaculada Cercadillo Torrecilla, CEIP Gabriel García Márquez, Getafe, Madrid; Paco Sansaloni Felis, CEIP Cervantes, Gandía, Valencia; Patricia Meneses Dekker, Escola Esteve Barrachina, Sitges, Barcelona; Teresa Rofes Bauzá, Escola Barcelona, Barcelona.

The authors and publishers would like to thank the following for permission to reproduce their photographs:
Alamy/Andrew Aitchison pp34(4), 83(c), Alamy/Blend Images p74(tc), Alamy/ Bon Appetit p30(cr), Alamy/The Art Archive p45(tcl), Alamy/SimonBelcher p106(br), Alamy/Prisma Bildagentur AG p15(waterfall), Alamy/blickwinkel p30(cmr), Alamy/PearlBucknall pp64(1), p86(2), Alamy/eye35 pp34(8), 83(e), Alamy/Gaertner p62(bcr), Alamy/Juniors Bildarchiv GmbH p20(3), Alamy/David Hastilow p50(tm), Alamy/Helga pp64(5), 86(10), Alamy/ Louise Heusinkveld p20(2), Alamy/Steffan Hill p74(b), Alamy/Cindy Hopkins pp14(9), 81(7), Alamy/D. Hurst pp44(7), 64(10), 84(a), 86(3), Alamy/Imagestate pp14(8), 81(2), Alamy/Interfoto p118(a), Alamy/Kuttig—RF—Kids p5(cl), Alamy/Art Kowalsky pp14(3), 81(5), Alamy/Aliaksandr Mazurkevich p84(g), Alamy/MITO Images p74 (tr), Alamy/Keith Morris p10(cl), Alamy/Sean O'Neill p55(bcr), Alamy/James Osmond p110(l), Alamy/ scenicireland.com/Christopher Hill Photographic p35(bcr), Alamy/David R. Frazier Photolibrary, Inc pp34(7), 83(h), Alamy/Craig Joiner Photography pp34(10), p83(f), Alamy/ Colin Palmer Photography p34(9), Alamy/James Nesterwitz p41(tmr), Alamy/Big Cheese Photo LLC p62(tcr), Alamy/Buzz Pictures p72(tcr), Alamy/Aliaksandr Mazurkevich p44(5), Alamy/MBI p74(tcl), Alamy/Jeff Morgan 05 pp34(6), 83(b), Alamy/NASA 118(e), Alamy/Colin Palmer Photography p83(a), Alamy/Phil Rees p108(br), Alamy/Rtimages pp64(8), 88(5), Alamy/Frans Lanting Studio p20(1), Alamy/Jack Sullivan p108(bm), Alamy/Superstock pp14(4), 81(3), Alamy/Eye Ubiquitous pp44(10), 84(e), Alamy/Finnbarr Webster pp45(bcr), 96(cr); **Brand X Pictures** pp14(10), 81(1); **COMSTOCK IMAGES** p30(cm); **Corbis** pp32(cl), 64(9), 86(6), 104(bm), Corbis/a.collectionRF/amanaimages pp24(5), 82(5), Corbis/Heide Benser p9(l), 15(bl), 35(l), 42(bl), 48(bl), 52(bl), 59(l), 72(bl), Corbis/Bettmann p49(tm), Corbis/Hulton-Deutsch Collection pp45(bcl), 79(tr), Corbis/ Hero Images Inc p55 (c), Corbis/Kang Kim/Gallery Stock/Galeries p32(cr), Corbis/ Joe Toth/BPI p11(footballer), Corbis/Matthias Hiekel/dpa p10(cm), Corbis/KidStock/ Blend Images pp9(r), 15(br), 35(r), 42(br), 48(br), 52(br), 59(r), 72(br), Corbis/Radius Images p15(cr), Corbis/Lew Robertson p82(7), Corbis/TEK IMAGE/Science Photo Library p64(6), Corbis/Wieder, Frank/the food passionates pp24(9), 82(4), Corbis/Lew Robertson p24(10), Corbis/Creativ Studio Heinemann/Westend61 p24(1), Corbis/Steve Vidler pp34(2), 83(g), Corbis/Creativ Studio Heinemann/Westend61 p82(1); Digital Vision p104(cr); **FLPA**/Mike Perry/Minden Pictures p18(cr); **Getty Images** pp24(4, 8), pp35(cr), 60 (tcr, cl, bcl, cr), 79(tl), 79(tm), 82(9,10), 102, 106(cr), Getty Images/AFP p34(3), 72(tcl), 83(j), Getty Images/Hulton Archive p53(tcl), Getty Images/Alistair Berg p5(cr), Getty Images/Mark Bowden p62(tcl), Getty Images/Zero Creatives p5(bcl), Getty Images/ Creative Crop p31(cmr), Getty Images/Stuart Dee p96(b), Getty Images/Thierry Dosogne pp34(5), 83(i), Getty Images/Vladimir Godnik p42(tcl), Getty Images/Rick Gomez pp2(bl),8(cl),12(br),19(bl), 25(bl), 39(l), 45(bl), 55(br), 62(br), 69(l), Getty Images/Steve Gorton pp64(2), 86(1), Getty Images/Robert Harding pp14(2), 81(9), Getty Images/Brand New Images p106(c), Getty Images/Juanmonino p30(tcl), Getty Images/Kristin Lee pp24(2), 82(3), Getty Images/Doug McKinlay p35(tcr), Getty Images/Jose Moya p50(tl), Getty Images/Maximilian Stock Ltd pp24(3), 82(8), Getty Images/Robert Decelis Ltd p60(c), Getty Images/Stuart Pearce p8(tr), Getty Images/Time & Life Pictures pp52(bcl), p118(d), Getty Images/Yellowdog Productions p62(bcl), Getty Images/Sami Sarkis p63(insert), Getty Images/Image Source pp5(bcr), 24(7), 82(2), Getty Images/ Bluemoon Stock pp64(4), p86(8), Getty Images/Lucidio Studio, Inc. p32(cm), Getty Images/ Maria Teijeiro p21(tcr), Getty Images/David Tipling p21(cr), Getty Images/UIG p50(cl), Getty Images/Tom Pfeiffer/VolcanoDiscovery pp14(1), p81(6), Getty Images/Ingmar Wesemann pp14(5), 81(10), Getty Images/yellowdog p55(bcl); **Image 100** pp30(cl), 104(bl); **Imagesource** pp18(tr), 42(bcl, bcm), 44(6), 63(tm, tr), 84(j), 110(r), Image Source/ Corbis pp47, 50(cm), 52(bcr), Image Source/Moodboard pp34(1), p83(d); **Johnson & Johnson** p49(tl); **Macmillan Australia** pp64(7), 86(9), **Macmillan South Africa** pp97, 104(tr), **Macmillan Publishers/Stuart Cox** pp 2(tr), 3(cl), 4, 6, 10(t), 10(b), 11(t), p12(t), 13(t), 14(tl), 16, 20(tl, b), 21(t), 23(t), 24(tl), 24(6), 25(t), 30(t, b), 31(t), 32(t), 33(t), 34(t), 35(t), 36(t), 40(t, b), 41(t), 42(t), 51(tm), 52(t), 53(t), 54, 55(t), 55(tcl), 56, 60(t), 60(bm), 61(t), 62(tm), 63(tl), 64(t), 65(t), 66(t), 68(r, l), 70(t), 71(t), 72(t), 73(t), 74(t), 74(bcm), 75(tcl, bcm), 76(cr,b); **Mark Ormerod** p25(cake); **MARS** p44(1.2), p61(b), p70(tcr), p108(bl) ; **Photodisc** p33(cr), **PhotoDisc/Getty Images** pp104(br), 106(tr); **Photoshot**/Martin Ciesielski p25(palm), Photoshot/The Irish Image Collection p40(cr), Photoshot/UPPA p48(tm), Photoshot/ChinaFotoPress/Gu Yue p53(tcl, insert), **Photoshot/Steve Vidler** p108(bl); **REX**/Underwood Archives p52(cl), REX/Canadian Press p60(bcr); **Science Source** p45(tcr); **Shutterstock**/eurobanks pp3(cr), 44(tl), 45(t), 46(t), 50(t, bm), Shutterstock/Ken Durden p11(football game), Shutterstock/Dorti p11(stadium), Shutterstock/Jeff Schultes p11(concert), Shutterstock/Ken Wolter pg18(tl), Shutterstock/Elena Rostunova p21(br), Shutterstock/Vorontsova Anastasiia p31(br), Shutterstock/Marian Weyo p41(bmr), Shutterstock/Carl Stewart p43 insert, (tml), Shutterstock/Ingus Kruklitis p43(insert, tmr), Shutterstock/Katherine Welles p61(bcr), Shutterstock/KucherAV p51(tmr), Shutterstock/ Sean Pavone p61(tcr), Shutterstock/RomeoLu p70(tcl), Shutterstock/Anton_Ivanov p70(bml), Shutterstock/Tim Stirling p70(bmr), Shutterstock/digishoots p73 (tcr, insert), Shutterstock/Ondrej Chvatal p108(br), Shutterstock/Ondrej Chvatal p108(br), Shutterstock/Robnroll p108(bm); **Stockbyte** pp44(3), 84(f); **Superstock**/Album/Prisma/ Album 118(b), Superstock/Eye Ubiquitous p76(tl), Superstock/Food and Drink p30(bcl), SuperStock/Blend Images pp2(br), 8(cr), 12(bl), 19(br), 25(br), 39(r), 45(bl), 49(br), 55(bl), 62(bl), 69(r), Superstock/Axiom Photographic/Design Pics p75(b), Superstock/Pixtal p52 (tcm), Superstock/Stockbroker/Purestock p51(tr), Superstock/Superstock p75 (tl); **Thinkstock**/BananaStock p10(cr), Thinkstock/german-images p121(1), Thinkstock/ istock pp 14(6, 7), 19(tl, tr), 31(t), 42(tcm), 44(1), 44(4), 44(8), 64(3), 81(8,4), 84(i), 84(c), 84(b), 86(7), 106(b), Thinkstock/JaySi p5(bcl), Thinkstock/Jupiterimages p74(tl), Thinkstock/ OlgaMiltsova p31(c); Thinkstock/Purestock p8(tl), Thinkstock/moodboard p106(a), Thinkstock/Photodisc p19(tml), Thinkstock/Pixand p42(tcr), Thinkstock/Ryan McVay p74 (tr), Thinkstock/Stockbyte p19(tmr); Thinkstock/Valua Vitaly p74(t); Thinkstock/Up the Resolution p30(tcl); **Wham-O** p49(tr); **Yorkshire Sculpture Park**/Barbara Hepworth, Squares With Two Circles, 1963. Courtesy Tate © Bowness, Hepworth Estate.

Commissioned photography by Stuart Cox: pp2(t, c), 4(tl, tr, b), 5(b), 11(b), 13(cr, cl), 23(cl), 33(b), 41(b), 43(b), 53(br), 63(br), 65(b), 66(1—4), 67(5—9), 71(b), 73(br), 79(br, bl).
Author photograph (Carol Read) by Michael Selley

Printed and bound in Thailand

2021 2020 2019 2018 2017
10 9 8 7 6 5 4 3 2 1